Adulting for Beginners

Life Skills for Adult Children, Teens, High School and College Students

Contents

Introduction

Becoming an adult is incredibly exciting. We have freedom to choose how and where we will live our lives. It could be a time of exploring college options for some, while first jobs may be on the horizon for others. Whatever your case, if you are in your late teens and 20s, this is when you develop yourself, build your strengths, and work on your weaknesses. Because with greater freedom, comes greater responsibilities - not to mention a TON of new skills you'll need to master as a grown-up!

As an adult you have so many more choices. You can decide what and when to eat, where to live, and what time to go to bed. School taught you a lot, but there were many others that you will have to learn on your own. Maybe you can tell me what the capital of Estonia is, the stages of the water cycle, and the square root of 144. But none of those things will bc helpful when you blow a tire, have trouble with your first landlord, or show an allergic reaction when living alone.

This is because adulting is not easy. It can be super challenging. And what we learn in high school, even though it is important, rarely gives us the answers to our everyday struggles when we start to be an "adult". We must deal with taxes, deadlines, laundry, eating healthy, exercising, getting enough sleep, etc. So it is ok to feel lost and overwhelmed at times. But the good news is that you're in the right place. We're going to cover all your adulting questions like.... How do I apply for a job? What should I wear to an interview? How do I choose where to live? When do I know fruit has gone bad? Where have all my socks gone?!

In the next pages, all your questions will be answered. You'll learn not only how to survive in a grown up world, but how to be a super successful adult too. So let's get started!

Part 1: Life skills & living away from home

One of the biggest changes you'll encounter is moving away from home. Most of us will move away at some point, for college or work. But how do you find the right home for you? What should you consider? Let's begin with a few important things to consider.

1.   Renting

To successfully rent your first home, you must take several steps.

Choosing your location

The initial step when deciding where to get your first apartment/house is to choose zones of the city you like and discard those that you know won't fit your needs. Here are some things you should consider:

- Is it near shops or supermarkets? Can you walk to these or do you need a car?

- What about public transportation and parking spaces? Is there a place to park outside? Is it designated or how exactly does it work? Is your new home near a train station or bus stop?

- Are there bars around the area? If you're a party animal this might be perfect. But if you work shifts, you might not appreciate loud party noises late at night.

- Are you near parks, gyms, and other leisure places you consider important?

- Is it safe? Remember to check this at night also. You can best get to know a neighborhood by walking around it.

- How long will it take for you to travel each day to your work or college? If you hate commuting, you might need to find somewhere within walking distance. Or are you willing to live further away for a lower rent, but have a longer commute?

More than one area of your city is likely to fit your criteria for where you want to live, so the next consideration is the distance from your work/college.

Defining your budget

Knowing your budget is essential before choosing an apartment. The cost of renting will not only include rent, but also internet, food, transportation, heat, and other expenses.

In terms of a renting budget, the 30% rule is often used. According to this rule, we should spend no more than 25%/30% of our income on rent and expenses. Rent, services (gas, electricity, water, internet), and taxes will be included. Using this rule, you'll ensure you have enough money for your everyday expenses, such as food and transportation.

After determining how much rent you can afford, decide whether you will live alone or with a roommate and what type of apartment you will live in. In many cities, renting an entire apartment is incredibly expensive, so renting a room in a shared apartment may be the only option for many people.

Sharing vs. living alone

After reviewing your budget and clarifying how much you can spend on rent, you can choose what kind of home you would like to live in.

Determining how many bedrooms and bathrooms the apartment should have will depend mostly on whether you'll live alone or with someone else.

If the apartment is just for yourself, there are two things to have in mind: storage and working space. First, does the apartment have enough storage space for your things? And on the other hand, will you be working from home? If that's the case, it would be good if you considered an extra space so you can have a comfortable working area.

There is also the possibility that you decide to share the apartment with someone else. If that is the case, remember to prioritize big common spaces and a comfortable room for yourself. Whenever you share a house, your room becomes your space, so try to make it something you'd enjoy spending time in.

Sharing can be a great experience or a terrible one depending on how it is organized. It would be frustrating to wake up late for work and find there are two people in line ahead of you to take a shower. Crazy as that may sound, it happens more often than you think. The ideal situation would be for two people to share a toilet and three to share a shower.

 But sharing an apartment can also be the best decision ever, and a way to make lifelong friends.

Viewing the apartment

When you're viewing the house or apartment, there are a few things to keep in mind.

- First, get an overall impression of the house. Is it clean and light? Is there any mold on the walls? Is the kitchen a mess?

Does it look like the people who live there care about it? Walking into a dirty dark apartment is not a great start.

- If you will be sharing, find out who lives there now. Are they all college students who love to party? Are they professionals who work a lot? Are the people who stay there during the week but are not there much at the weekend?

- What is the situation with having friends or girlfriends/boyfriends over?

- What is the landlord like? Does he come around often? Is he good at getting things fixed when they break?

- What type of contract is required?

- Is a deposit needed and if yes, how much?

Signing the contract

Rental contracts usually require you to give the landlord a warranty concerning your ability to pay the rent in the future. Depending on the circumstances, you may be required to provide your income statements or a guarantor. You can always call a real estate office to find out the usual expectations regarding rental contracts in your city.

Finding the right home for you is not impossible, and the effort will pay off. With these simple steps, you will get a house that not only meets your needs but also does not stretch you financially. Once you're in it, it's a whole new chapter.

2. Moving in

After you have successfully rented your apartment (or room in a house share) and are satisfied with the results, the time has come to fill it up. If you are in a room share situation, you might only need to buy some of these - mainly things for your own room. If you are renting a house by yourself, you might need to invest in more items.

As general advice, buy consciously. If you don't want to find yourself in a year covered with stuff you don't use, buying consciously is essential. These are some points to keep in mind when shopping.

Buying furniture

Start with buying only the essentials. A piece of furniture to sleep on, another to sit on, to dine, etc. Here are some items to consider:

The bed

People's health depends on the quality of their sleep, as you know. We spend roughly a third of our lives sleeping. Would you want to spend that much time sleeping in an uncomfortable bed? The mattress market offers an enormous variety of options. Special foam is used in modern models that are incredibly durable and do not easily lose shape.

For the bed's structure, a simple one is always the best. Investing in a classic bed frame of neutral colors that will last a lifetime is a great idea. And by changing the duvet or pillows in your room, you can transform the look of it. In addition, it is also important to think about how much storage space you need. Also think how you will get this bed to your bedroom. Can it be moved in a few pieces? Will it fit up the stairs to your apartment? Don't forget to consider the logistics when you've found your super comfy bed!

Once you know the size of your bed, then you'll also need sheets, pillows, pillow covers and either a duvet or blankets that match your bed size. Two of each is a good idea as you can use one set while the other set is in the wash.

Sofa

Since we spend most of our time in the living room, the sofa is like the heart of the house. Our sofas are more relevant than we think, whether watching movies or TV shows, getting together with friends, or relaxing after work.

As with the bed, the recommendation is to choose neutral colors and a classic design so you don't have any problems changing the apartment's decor in the future. A sofa with a washable cover is a great idea too.

Storage

The fastest way to declutter your home or bedroom, is to buy some storage units and tidy things up. Buying one or two useful storage units for your home is one of the most practical and useful things you can do!

The best place to buy furniture

When buying your first pieces of furniture, Flat pack furniture is what I recommend you go for.

The first thing that stands out about this type of furniture is that it is the most affordable you can get on the market. This is because their large-scale production makes them cheaper and easier to manufacture. Additionally, they're cheaper because they compensate for their lower durability, but if you take care of them, they'll last a long time.

Shipping, assembly, and disassembly are easy. Because customers pick their furniture and build it in their homes, companies don't have to pay huge shipping costs.

It is possible to customize flat packs, there are numerous websites and hacks that can be used to improve or change the design. By doing so, people can make a cheap flat-pack look more expensive and luxurious for very little money.

Packing and moving this type of furniture is easy. You can easily transport your furniture and reassemble it when you move house by disassembling it, packing it in its flat boxes, and putting it in the moving truck.

· Extra: Kitchen implements

In the kitchen, you'll need the utensils for day-to-day use, things like plates, cutlery, and glasses. Even though these are important, the good news is you don't have to spend too much on them. The first days after moving would be tough without these things, so they should be a priority.

Now that we have your bedroom sorted and kitchen items ready, the supermarket is the next place you should visit.

Your first grocery shop

When you get home the first time, you'll need to visit the grocery store immediately since the fridge and pantry are empty. Here's some advice for making your first grocery shop a success.

Set a budget for the purchase

The key to saving personal finances is to know how much money you can or should spend on the shopping basket. It will be much easier for you to control spending and waste if you create a budget for food, whether it is monthly, weekly, or daily.

Prepare your shopping list before you go grocery shopping.

Adding more than you need to your shopping basket can make your grocery bill skyrocket. If you haven't planned your purchase, it is easier for this to happen. Before shopping, check your pantry and think about the meals you will prepare for that week, so you will know what you need. Once you have a list of all these items, limit yourself to buying only the items on it. This way, you will avoid getting too carried away by cravings and spontaneously buying unnecessary things.

Buy at the cheapest supermarket

The store you make your purchase may impact your spending more than you realize. It is important to understand that when identifying the cheapest supermarkets, it is about finding the best prices (which saves you money), not the one with the most offers. Ask your friends or work colleagues to find some good value supermarkets in your area, or check what's close by on Google maps.

Try using an online supermarket price comparator

The advantage of shopping online is that you don't have to go to the supermarket. When you don't have to navigate endless aisles of items, you're more likely to stick with the products you need.

Furthermore, it is also easier to compare their prices and choose the one with a lower price. There are several online supermarket comparators to help you with this.

Buy seasonal goods

You can save on your purchase by purchasing seasonal products since they are cheaper.

When the climatic conditions are right for their cultivation, they can be produced easily and supplied in greater abundance, lowering their price.

Check best before dates

Food usually has a limited life span. So check the date on all food items before you purchase. There's no point buying lots of chicken if it will all be out of date tomorrow. But if you know you will be eating your food the same day, sometimes you can get good bargains on items that are coming up to their use by date.

Give White Labels a Chance

It's well-known that white brands are less expensive, so purchasing them at the supermarket will save you money. Even though private label products tend to cost less, some nutrition experts advise against them. The best way to ensure the quality of these items is to always check the ingredients.

Use coupons and loyalty cards to save money.

Getting a loyalty card can be a good idea since shopping is almost inevitable, and you tend to go to the same shops almost every day. Their members are provided with certain benefits, such as the classic coupons they can use to get items at a better price.

Avoid prepared products

You will generally pay more for precooked and prepared dishes than if you bought the ingredients separately.

Items such as tomato sauce, grated cheese, cut vegetables, etc., are similarly affected. This is a common selection of products in a shopping basket, but the truth is that they will raise your final bill more than if you buy fresh tomatoes, cheese, or vegetables and prepare them yourself.

Buy in bulk

Sometimes, we come across large packages containing many units of the same product and think they are too big and take up too much space. This is a shame because large formats are usually cheaper.

This can be solved by sharing it with someone, like your neighbor, family member, or friend. It's also a good idea to buy items in bulk that you can store and use over time, like toilet paper or cleaning products. This will only take up a little space.

Compare prices per kilo or per liter, not per unit

By taking advantage of the fact that usually, the largest format is typically the cheapest, some chains put higher prices on packages with more units, even when they can theoretically save money. To avoid this, it is important to check the cost per unit/liter/kilo, which is expressed in smaller letters on the same price tag.

Beware of items near the checkout

You will often find attractive products such as trinkets or magazines at the checkout stand and practical items such as light bulbs or batteries. Since these items are not very expensive, they are easy to add to a basket in a last-minute impulse purchase while waiting for payment. It will cost you a few more dollars to do this.

Have fun with your first shop! The most important thing is to remember that every mistake when living alone is an opportunity to learn and buy better in the future. In a few days, keep a note of what you forgot to buy, or what you didn't buy enough of, and update your weekly shopping list with this info. This will save you time and hassle in the future and streamline your shopping each week. You can also see if any stores do free online delivery, and save some extra time by ordering your food to be delivered each week.

Basic grocery list

A list is an essential tool we must have at hand when going to the supermarket because it will help us plan and control the expenses incurred to stock up on food, utensils, and cleaning products for home and personal use. Not having a shopping list often leads to impulse purchases and forgetting the important stuff.

The following is a compilation of basic products, there is no need to buy them all, but you can create a list of what you need and make it as detailed and accurate as possible.

Groceries

- EGGS

- PASTA (SPAGHETTI, LASAGNA, PENNE, ETC.)

- BAGGED SOUPS (STARS, LETTERS, ETC.)

- BOXED CEREAL

- WHEAT FLOUR

- CORNMEAL

- PANCAKE FLOUR

- GROUND BREAD

- MAYONNAISE

- MUSTARD
- BOXED MASHED POTATOES
- VEGETABLE OIL
- OLIVE OIL
- COOKING SPRAY
- VINEGAR
- CHOCOLATE POWDER
- CHOCOLATE BARS
- JELLIES
- BAKING SODA
- JAMS
- COOKIES
- HOT SAUCE
- WORCESTERSHIRE SAUCE
- SOY SAUCE
- TOMATO SAUCE
- DRESSINGS

Beverages

- WATER (PLAIN, FLAVORED, WITH GAS)

- SOFT DRINKS

- JUICES

- TEA (POWDER, SACHET, OR BREW)

Fruits and vegetables

- SPINACH

- LETTUCE

- CABBAGE

- PARSLEY

- CILANTRO

- BELL PEPPER

- BROCCOLI

- GARLIC

- ONION

- MUSHROOMS

- SERRANO PEPPER

- ANCHO PEPPER

- TOMATO

- TOMATO

- POTATO

- CARROT

- PUMPKIN OR ZUCCHINI

- CELERY

- TAMARIND

- SEASONAL FRUIT

- LEMON

- APPLE

- WATERMELON

- BANANAS

- AVOCADO

- PAPAYA

- ORANGE

- RED FRUITS

- CUCUMBER

- PLUMS

- BLUEBERRIES

Cooking essentials

- REFINED SALT

- GRAIN SALT

- PEPPER

- GARLIC POWDER

- OREGANO

- CINNAMON

- THYME

- ROSEMARY

- PAPRIKA

- TURMERIC

- ACHIOTE

- CUMIN

- SAFFRON

- CHICKEN BOUILLON CUBES

- BEEF BOUILLON CUBES

- BASIL

- VANILLA

- DRIED LAUREL

- CHILI POWDER

Canned food

- TUNA

- SARDINES

- BEANS TO TASTE

- POWDERED MILK

- CONDENSED MILK

- EVAPORATED MILK

- CHIPOTLES

- RAJAS

- VEGETABLES

- CORN FLAKES AND

- FRUITS IN SYRUP

Grains and cereals

- BEANS

- RICE

- LENTILS

- OATS

- FLAXSEED

- CORN

Meat, chicken, fish and seafood

- STEAK

- CHOPS AND GROUND BEEF (PORK OR BEEF)

- CUTS OF BEEF TO TASTE

- LAMB

- CHICKEN BREAST

- CHICKEN THIGH AND LEG

- FISH FILET

- SHRIMP

- SALMON

- PORK OR TURKEY HAM

- PORK OR TURKEY SAUSAGE

- BACON

Sausages and dairy

- MILK

- SOY MILK

- ALMOND MILK;

- CHEESE

- CREAM CHEESE

- SOUR CREAM

- BUTTER

- MARGARINE

- CHORIZO

- SALAMI

Personal maintenance

- TOILET SOAP

- SHAMPOO

- CONDITIONER

- HAIR GEL

- DEODORANT

- SANITARY NAPKINS

- TOILET PAPER

- TOOTHPASTE

- TOOTHBRUSH

- BODY AND FACE CREAM

- SHAVING FOAM

- RAZOR AND RAZOR BLADES

- DIAPERS

- DISPOSABLE TISSUES AND

- MAKEUP

General cleaning and others

- NAPKINS

- ABSORBENT TOWELS

- ALUMINUM FOIL

- PLASTIC WRAP

- GARBAGE BAGS

- FIBER AND SPONGE FOR DISHES

- DISHWASHING SOAP

- DEGREASER

- BROOM

- DUSTPAN

- BUCKET

- JARS

- RAGS

- LAUNDRY SOAP (LIQUID, POWDER, OR BAR)

- DRAIN CLEANER

- FLOOR CLEANER

- CHLORINE

- GLASS CLEANER

- LIGHT BULBS

- CANDLES

- MATCHES AND/OR LIGHTER

- BATTERIES

- GLOVES

Once you've got a complete grocery list, you can go shopping knowing that nothing is missing from your house when you get home. Remember, buy frozen and refrigerated foods last.

Cleaning basics

One of your roles as an adult is not - cleaning! And you're about to find out that there are about a million different household cleaning products. Dust cleaners, window cleaners, all-purpose cleaners, floor cleaners, disinfectors, and degreasers are available for all sorts of uses. But is it really necessary to spend so much on them, or is it just a matter of accumulating unnecessary cans?

Cleaning products

To keep each area of your house in perfect condition, including the dishes, stove, furniture, and others, you will need the necessary utensils. Many cleaning products are unnecessary, so let's go through the ones that are necessary and why.

The basics

Depending on your type of floor (tiles, carpet, lino or wood), you will have to get a product that helps you keep it in perfect condition. Brooms, dustpans, and mop buckets are a good place to start.

Gloves, rags, and fibers to consider

- A soft cloth (better microfiber) to clean the dust.

- A cloth for cleaning the kitchen, one for the countertop every day and another for the hob.

- In the bathroom, you need a pair, one for the toilet and another for the rest of the fixtures and surfaces.

- An extra one to clean window panes, for example, might be a good idea.

- When cleaning, don't forget to protect your hands. Gloves are always helpful.

Kitchen products to consider

- Dishwasher detergent or dishwasher machine detergent (specific to this appliance). Add polish and salt if you live in an area with hard water.

- Disinfectant (antibacterial) for cooking surfaces. Ammonia and water for tiles.

- Clean hoods and other areas with degreaser.

- Floor cleaner liquid

- Window cleaner

- Antibacterial surface cleaner

Laundry products to consider

- A good detergent and softener for your clothes.

- Specific products for removing sweat stains and odors.

Bathroom products

- A specific cloth for the toilet area.

- WC bleach and a cleaning agent that won't damage the enamel of the toilets or the taps (use a soft cloth, not a scouring pad).

- An anti-limescale cleaning spray can be used to remove stubborn stains on shower screens.

- Glass cleaners work better on mirrors.

- For the floor, a water-diluted floor cleaner.

Cleaning routine

The key to a happy life is a tidy home; dividing the cleaning into daily, weekly, and monthly tasks is easy to achieve. Organizing your tasks according to how often they should be done will help you avoid forgetting anything. Here is a sample cleaning schedule.

Daily cleaning

There are a few things you have to do every day. You should place clean utensils in cabinets and drawers in the kitchen, then dirty dishes should be cleaned or put in the dishwasher if you have one. Using this method, your sink will always be clear.

You will also need to clean leftover food with a scourer or a cloth so that they do not accumulate and end up smelling unpleasant later. After that, clean the countertop and glass ceramic and vacuum if necessary.

Make sure the living room is tidy, pick up newspapers, books, empty coffee cups or magazines that are strewn about.

Open the bedroom windows in the morning to ventilate and pick up any clothes or shoes on the floor. Finally, air out the sheets and bedspreads. Make sure to store them in the corresponding drawers and cabinets; when you do this daily, you will always have everything perfectly arranged.

Although the bathroom needs to be deep cleaned every week, you should superficially clean it every day. This involves passing over the sink, the toilet, the shower, and the screens more than anything else.

Taking out the garbage daily will also be necessary, especially if it is organic, to prevent it from smelling. The inorganics will also be disposed of every few days, along with the glass and cardboard, in their respective containers.

Weekly cleaning

Consider taking advantage of a couple of hours on weekends to thoroughly clean the house so that it remains in perfect condition throughout the week. Unlike daily cleaning, weekly cleaning requires thoroughness and dedication.

With daily cleaning, the kitchen will stay clean, but you have to vacuum and mop all corners of the floor every week. Additionally, it will be time to focus on appliances used daily and are easy to clean, such as the oven or microwave. By passing a cloth with a special product inside both appliances, you can prevent them from getting too dirty and prolong their useful life. It will also be necessary to give the exterior of the extractor kitchen a pass during the weekly cleaning, reserving the interior for the monthly cleaning.

In the living room, it's time to shake out the blankets and pillows as well as vacuum and dust the table, bookcase and shelves. You can also take this opportunity to clean out newspapers, magazines, and old papers that you no longer need and that get in the way. Fresh flowers will brighten your week when you put them in a vase.

It is also important to thoroughly clean the bathroom, paying particular attention to the shower tiles, the mirror, and the floor. Following the daily cleaning plan, you won't have to spend too much time cleaning the sink, shower, and toilet.

You might consider putting your dirty clothes in the washing machine over the weekend. Washing the towels and changing the sheets every week is also recommended. Additionally, if you iron clean clothes once a week, you will prevent them from accumulating.

Dust all surfaces and shelves in the house with the vacuum while not forgetting the door frames and paintings that hang on the walls.

Monthly cleaning

According to many experts, certain appliances should be thoroughly cleaned at least once a month. By doing so, they can be kept in good working order for a longer period of time.

Extractor hoods must be disassembled and cleaned inside and out with hot water and steam, as well as the filters with anti-grease products. To prevent limescale and dirt accumulation, it is also important to wash the washing machine and the dishwasher periodically. Many models offer a special program for washing the appliance.

You may also want to review the fridge in great detail. Remove all expired food from the fridge and throw it away. After this, clean the interior and trays of the freezer to remove any leftovers, and make sure you go over the freezer.

Both inside and outside of window panes need to be cleaned regularly. The market offers a wide range of products suitable for this purpose and special tools that are enhanced to make your work easier.

Season cleaning

As the seasons change, it is time for a more specific cleaning, such as wardrobe changes: putting away the clothes you no longer need and bringing out the ones you'll start using.

If you have plants, you can also take the opportunity to prune them and remove dead leaves. If you have a garden, it is time to remove the leaves and branches, clean the weeds, and do not hesitate to give it a new look by planting fresh flowers.

If it is present, a parquet must be properly maintained to keep its beautiful appearance. Pass the mop over the floor using the products specifically designed for this type of flooring, then apply a layer of wax to make it look shinier.

Annual cleaning

Spend one or two days yearly on areas of the house that don't typically get cleaned very often but where dirt accumulates.

As for the kitchen, remove any packages or cans of food that have passed their expiration dates from the cupboards and discard them. After cleaning, use a cloth and soap to clean the surface thoroughly. Continue cleaning the cabinets and drawers where you store your plates, glasses, and cutlery. Make sure you do not overlook any corner.

Remove all the clothes from your closets, both in the rooms and the hallways, and put all the clothes and shoes you don't use in boxes to donate or throw them out if they are in poor shape. Additionally, while the wardrobe and its shelves are empty, make sure to clean them thoroughly. The best time to do this cleaning is during the summer or winter wardrobe change.

If your curtains or blinds are made of fabric, you can wash them in the washing machine and air out your carpets, mattresses, and pillows. If something does not fit in the washing machine, you can wash it in the bathtub or take it to a dry cleaner.

3. Laundry, house maintenance tips & more

Doing laundry

Knowing how to wash clothes in the washing machine is the first step to keeping clothes looking new for a longer period and also extending the life of your washing machine. The secret is to avoid a few mistakes that we make due to ignorance or routine, and we will save time, resources, and, in the end, money.

Avoid these five laundry mistakes:

1) Overfilling the washing machine with clothes. The drum should be filled a little more than three-quarters, with your hand fitting between the clothes and the drum walls. If you fill it too much, the clothes may not stir well enough and may not come out clean.

2) Ignoring the purpose of each compartment for detergent, fabric softener, and bleach. It is essential to pour each product in its place to avoid blending, which can ruin fabrics. You should also follow the level signals and not overdose.

3) Adding more detergent than necessary and not selecting the right washing cycle. Dose according to the manufacturer's instructions based on the dirtiness and hardness of the water. By adding more product, you are not washing better. On the contrary, traces of detergent or fabric softener may remain on the clothes, so you will need to rewash them. If your clothes are lightly soiled, wash them in short cycles and cold water; if they are very soiled, wash them in longer and higher temperatures.

4) Do not classify clothes before washing them. For the best cleaning, separate the garments by color (white, color, black) and similar fabrics.

5) Not reading labels (especially if it is a new garment). Labels inform us about temperatures; machine, dry or hand wash; bleach tolerance. Don't take anything for granted. If you are careless, you could ruin a garment. Here is a list of some common washing symbols you'll find on clothes:

- Machine wash

- Hand wash

- Do not wash

- Do not bleach

- Water temperature 30 degrees

- Iron

- Do not iron

- Tumble dry

- Drip dry

- Dry flat

- Dry clean

- Do not dry clean

How to boil an egg

This sounds simple but it's a very important life skill! If you can boil an egg you can make a very fast meal. So here is how to do it. Bring some water and a little salt to a boil in a pot. Make sure there is enough water to cover the egg.

Bring to the boil then reduce the heat to a gentle simmer for 3-5 minutes. Different people like different consistencies to their hard boiled egg. A 3 minute egg will still be a little runny. A 5 minutes egg will be less runny. Experiment with how you like your egg cooked.

You can also cool down your egg, and eat it later by soaking it in cold water for a little while, until it is cooler and then you can remove the shell.

How to know when food has gone off

Your senses can detect food spoilage as food becomes rancid or moldy when it spoils, and you can smell, taste, or see this before it becomes unsafe to eat. The general rule is that when food looks gone off, it is best to discard it. If in doubt, throw it out. Food poisoning is quite nasty and should be avoided. There are several things to look out for, including bad smells, slimy and greenish coatings, or mold on the surface. Very dark colors in the meat, soft skin in the fish, lumps in the flour, bruises or soft parts in the fruit and vegetables are signs that this food is in poor condition and should not be eaten.

How to iron a shirt

When ironing any part of the shirt, you should ensure that the fabric is well stretched. If you iron the wrinkle instead of removing it, you will worsen it.

Start at the inside of the shirt collar. Slide the iron over the wrinkled areas from one end to the other. Flip the shirt over and repeat the process. Lastly, fold in half and pass it through the iron several times.

Then, carefully stretch the shirt on the surface, and remove the wrinkles near the neck.

You can then iron the open cuffs by undoing the button so you don't have a line in the middle.

Next, you finish ironing the sleeves and accommodate the fabric by taking the sleeves by their internal seams and ensuring that both sides are flat before starting.

Then, iron the back, with the shirt open, and then the front.

Iron around the buttons rather than over them when ironing since you might burn and destroy them.

How to change the battery in a smoke alarm

The first thing you need to do is check the type of battery your detector uses. When you don't have the factory manual, you can google your device and see what battery it needs. Or after you remove the current battery and get another similar one.

Changing a battery requires you first to check if the detector is connected to an electricity network. If it is, you must disconnect the power from the network to work safely. Next, you must remove the smoke detector, usually by unrolling or sliding the cover, depending on the model. After you have opened it, you should identify where the battery is located and remove it. Pay attention to which way the battery is placed, as you must insert the new one the same way.

Make sure the battery you put in works before putting the cover back. Check to see if there is any light that indicates the equipment is on or if there is any sound that indicates it is already working. Put the cover back on the detector to finish. Never stay in a house without a working smoke detector, as it may save your life.

How to fix your toilet

A toilet can present several problems, so if you don't want to spend a lot of money calling a specialist, you should try fixing it yourself first.

One issue that can arise is the toilet getting blocked and not flushing anymore. This is usually because someone has put something they shouldn't down the toilet - like sanitary towels or wipes etc. Use a plunger a few times to loosen any materials that might be clogging the toilet.

If your toilet doesn't flush, also check the tank to see if it has enough water. Maybe it's a water issue. The handle on your toilet you push to get it to flush could also have broken. A common symptom is that water gushes out of the bowl, and in this case, you need to check whether the discharge mechanism or the water inlet mechanism has been damaged. In either case, the tank must be opened to check its contents.

You should fix the inlet mechanism if the water level is above the discharge level since it does not break when it should, and water continues to enter despite being full. On the other hand, if the water level is below the discharge level, the outlet mechanism must be faulty.

As plastic pieces are used daily, it is difficult to fix them once they break. It is important to identify which part of the equipment is broken in this case so that you do not have to replace everything. You can try adjusting its parts and position if you identify which part isn't working, but if you notice a broken part, the best solution is to replace the entire mechanism.

Part 2: Productivity, health and relationships

On a flight, when suddenly the cabin becomes depressurized, we are told to put on a mask first, then assist others, right? The same goes for your well-being in everyday life. Thinking about projects, relationships, jobs and long term goals is very difficult if you don't know how to take care of yourself on a day to day basis. A healthy mental and physical life, routines that fit your needs, and learning to create valuable relationships in which you can be yourself will provide a great foundation from which to grow and succeed.

1.   Health

The difference between "healthy" and "sick" was evident as a child. If a doctor and some medicine were involved, you were sick. The rest of the time, you are healthy. As you grow older, you realize that health is a little more complicated. Anxiety, stress, allergies, where do we put them? It's hard to draw the line.

That's why it is important to remember that health isn't just the absence of disease, it's also a state of physical, mental, and social well-being. And to live a healthy life, we need to prevent, not react.

The power of self-care

Self-care comprises all those habits and attitudes we can perform to preserve and improve our health daily.

Self-care is equal to training your muscles to prevent injury during a race. Making simple changes in your daily habits will strengthen your system and health. Here are some of the changes you can consider.

Eat real food

Make a variety of fruits, vegetables, proteins, and whole grains the foundation of your diet. Batch cooking and an organized kitchen will help you achieve this.

Be consistent about when you eat. Skipping meals is not healthy long term, causing you to consume far more food than is necessary at the next meal, or snacking on unhealthy options. Considering our pace of life today, this can sometimes seem difficult, but it's something you need to prioritize.

Between meals, avoid snacking, or choose healthy snacks, such as non-fried nuts or fruit that provide essential nutrients.

Hydration is key. Besides helping to eliminate toxins, water aids digestion and prevents constipation. It is recommended to consume two liters of water each day.

Having a large bottle you can take with you everywhere and use as a measuring device to track how much water you drink is the easiest way to achieve this. Water, not soft drinks or sugary juices. In case you aren't used to drinking water regularly, adding a few slices of cucumber or lemon to your water bottle to flavor it can make it easier to drink.

Finally, nutrition must be cut back on very processed foods, which are high in trans or saturated fats, and consume foods with polyunsaturated fats, such as salmon, vegetable oil, nuts, or seeds. Don't forget, we truly are what we eat, so will you base your diet on junk food?

Sleep well

Getting rest is vital for our body to function properly. As well as affecting our hormonal, immune, and respiratory systems, poor sleep can also affect our blood pressure and cardiovascular health.

In addition, several investigations show that not sleeping can increase the risk of obesity, infections, and coronary diseases.

Sleeping well is more than just getting between 7 and 9 hours of sleep (the recommended hours of rest). It involves having a regular time to go to bed and wake up, having a bedtime routine (like brushing your teeth, taking a bath, or reading), and not drinking coffee or caffeinated beverages after 4 pm. Also, sleeping in comfortable clothes in a dark, quiet room is key.

If you find it difficult to fall asleep early and usually stay up late, there are two changes you can make. When the sun comes down, pause using screens and social media. They usually hyper-activate us, so if you use your phone less, you'll see how the need for resting appears. Also, try to have dinner two hours earlier than bedtime, and dim the lights after you do so. If you do this consistently, they will turn into signals for your body to know that resting time is coming soon and help it relax.

Move your body

A healthy lifestyle relies heavily on sport. If you think you do not have time or are not ready to start intense physical activity, you can start with baby steps, such as walking for short periods or stretching in the morning. Keep your muscles active by walking around. Make sure you get up every 60 minutes if you spend lots of time sitting.

Moderate long-term physical activity daily will bring many benefits, such as helping you control your blood sugar level, reducing the risk of coronary heart disease, promoting sleep quality, and increasing mindfulness in your body.

Over time you can increase the intensity of your sport. Learn to listen to your body. Don't force or strain your body. Wear equipment that is appropriate for the sport you practice. Good shoes and breathable clothing are essential.

Alcohol: Be careful

The annual death toll from alcohol worldwide is 3 million. The WHO reports the harmful effects of the abuse of alcohol, which is associated with over 200 pathologies and can lead to mental and behavioral disorders.

When it comes to consuming alcohol, moderation is key. Nutritionists and healthcare providers recommend limiting alcohol to social events or weekends, not over two units per event. Also, it is essential to drink water interspersed with alcohol.

If you drink alcohol during the week, do not have over one unit daily. The unit of drink constitutes a medium-sized beer or wine glass.

Be mindful of your hygiene

One of the good things COVID-19 has left us is the consciousness of the role of personal hygiene in preventing diseases. Good personal hygiene and cleanliness are a must, especially at home.

Washing your hands must be a part of your routine. This includes after traveling, before you eat, and after spending time with animals.

If you practice physical exercise or move around the city, it is good to shower daily to control germs that may affect your skin.

Also, changing your sheets and towels once a week will help you sleep in a clean environment and prevent allergies, skin breakouts, asthma, and other potential reactions related to the lack of regular cleaning.

Finally, if you live in the city, it is recommendable to incorporate the Asian custom of taking off your shoes and leaving them at the door when you get home. The pragmatic benefits are obvious: removing shoes keeps floors and carpets clean. But also, it will work as a reminder of the intention of keeping your home as a clean space.

Live slowly, prioritize mental health

As part of achieving physical health, mental health must also be considered. If one is not good, it will hurt the other and vice versa.

One of the main risks for our mental health today is stress. It is not only constantly present in our minds but drags us into loops of avoidance behaviors to "feel better," such as addictions, poorer diets, or sedentary life.

When it comes to taking care of your mental health, you can start by taking a few minutes off-line before starting your day. Connecting with what you feel, physically and emotionally, is key. Learn to accept yourself, and ask for help if you need it. Meditation is an excellent way to improve mental health and foster and nurture relationships with family and friends. Have one or more vital purposes for motivating yourself since having a long-term objective improves your mental health.

Self-care is less complicated than it seems. It is mainly about being conscious, being aware of what we put in our bodies (food, water, alcohol, screen time), and how we use it in our daily lives. Start by observing your everyday life to see what recommendations you could introduce to improve your well-being. Remember, "prevention is better than cure."

Health 101: Annual medical check-ups

When you get to your 20's, going to the doctor is on you. This means that it is your responsibility to take care of your health. Annual check-ups are the best way to ensure that we're healthy, treat diseases quickly, and keep our quality of life high.

After the summer, a check-up will show you how well you're doing so you can confidently return to your regular life. A complete medical check-up would include the following:

Clinical specialist

- Cholesterol control (if there are risk factors, otherwise they are done every five years)

- Diabetes screening (if risk factors present)

- Recommended vaccines

- Blood test

- Family history disease screenings

- Athletes: Examine the circulatory system and an electrocardiogram to detect anomalies related to sudden death.

Dermatologist

- Skin exam to check for lesions or moles that look suspicious

Sexual health specialist

- Men: Testicular exam

- Women: Pap smear, HPV vaccine, a breast exam.

- Screening for sexually transmitted infections (per patient request)

Mental health professional:

- If there's a history of emotional disorders, it is recommended.

Dentist:

- In time, you can solve cavities and gum problems.

Though it seems like a lot, it is only done once a year. Keep track of your health yearly, and there won't be any surprises. Through self-care and a yearly medical check-up, you will take the best approach to your health: prevention. As you improve your everyday habits, you will be confident that everything is going well by scheduling a check-up yearly.

If you're wondering if you win anything, the answer is; everything. Your body will be at its best, so you'll be closer to reaching your goals. The question is, what objectives are you setting for yourself?

2. Goal setting

If you are lost at sea, a map can be very useful, but you also need to know the name of the place you want to go to. The same thing happens in life. First we need to set our goals. What do we want to achieve in our career this year? What do we want to achieve in our personal lives in the next 12 months? What are our health goals for this year? When we know what our goals are, it's much simpler to then figure out a plan to get there.

SMART goals

Many adults spend their lives rushing from one job to another, from project to project, without ever feeling fulfilled by what they do. Usually, this happens because they accept what others ask them to do, rather than choosing their own direction for their life.

For example, I was a project manager in a tech company. I liked my job, but as the months passed, I became unhappy with the amount of overtime that was necessary.

During the summer, my boss called me into her office. She praised my work ethic, and said that if I continue on this path, there would be a promotion to senior project manager in my future, which would also include a raise in salary. Two months later, I had quit my job, as the small extra increase in salary, and a better job title would also have meant longer hours at the office and zero work life balance. But by knowing my life goals - to make a work life balance, and long term to move back to the country, saying no to a high profile job in the city was easy for me. And it was one of the best decisions I ever made.

SMART goals are an acronym that will guide your goal setting. Over time, you'll probably accomplish very little if you don't know where you want to go. Having clear ideas will turn into focused efforts and productive use of time and resources, increasing the chances of achieving what you want in life.

Specific: Your goals should be clear and focus on what you want. Simple and significant objectives are the ones we are looking for.

Measurable: We must measure how close we are to achieving our goals in order to make changes if necessary.

Attainable: The most common mistake when setting goals is aiming too high. Defining goals we can accomplish is basic for not feeling frustrated and giving up. Dividing the goals into smaller ones or in shorter periods is useful for achieving this. This doesn't mean we don't aim for the moon, we just start with baby steps on earth.

Realistic: Our goals should be something we can do. This does not equal an easy goal but an achievable one.

Time-oriented: The goals we set must be defined in time. This will clarify the processes and make it easier to understand the steps we must take to achieve what we want.

Using the SMART acronym when setting goals will help you gain clarity, focus, and motivation. Afterward, you should determine which goal matches your needs across the various areas of your life.

Divide and conquer: Goals by areas

There's a similar concept behind building an empire and creating who you want to be: divide and conquer. When setting goals, you need to identify what's important to you so you can create objectives that are consistent with what you value. A category distribution is a good system for goal setting. Here's some insight into different areas and some questions you can use to identify your goals.

Personal Development Goals

Personal and interpersonal skills are closely related to these types of objectives.

- What character traits would you like to develop?

- Are there any skills you want to master?

- What kind of friend do you want to be?

- What could you do for your physical well-being?

- Would you like to overcome your fear of public speaking?

- Would you like to be a better partner? Speak French? Or play the guitar?

As you can see, there are endless options for developing ourselves. Are languages, sports, and interpersonal skills you need to grow to be who you want to be?

Career/Financial Goals

Whether it's a career, business, or finances, these goals are related to what you want to have and be.

- Would you like to be a better leader and manage your teams better?

- What levels of financial abundance do you want to achieve?

- What position do you want to achieve in your company? Or do you want to become an entrepreneur and work for yourself?

- How much do you want to earn?

- Would you like to become the best salesperson in your company?

- If you are an entrepreneur or manager, what goals do you have for your organization?

- How far would you like to take it?

Adventure Objectives

There are two aspects to these goals - they are related to what you want to have and do on a playful level.

- What adventure and relaxed plan would you wish for most in the world?

- Travel to Australia?

- A house on the beach? A sailboat? A sports car?

- Stroll through New York?

- Go to a rock concert?

Contribution Objectives

These may be the most challenging and inspiring goals because this is your chance to make your mark on the world and "touch" other people's lives.

- Would you like to work at an NGO?

- Volunteering at a soup kitchen, helping to remove rubbish in your local area?

Once you have written down your SMART goals for each area of your life, it is time to return to the present. When setting them, we must remember that even though they are important, our goals are in the future, and the actual change occurs in the present. So, as we do with a compass, we look at them from time to time, so we don't get lost, but we get closer step by step.

In everyday life, those steps will bring us closer to our goals. Success is not an act but a habit.

3. Daily routines

Living alone - or even living with flatmates - can make time management somewhat problematic. We have all woken up five minutes before work starts. While it may happen occasionally, it's not a good way to impress your boss.

Living behind schedule always puts us in survival mode, far away from creativity and productivity. The best way to prevent this is to create a routine that fits your needs. Having a routine has solid benefits, like helping you grow personally, mentally, and pursue various goals.

If you don't have a routine yet, it is time to create one.

Discover your routine

When it comes to creating your routine, there are some things to take into consideration.

- Know what you want and why you want it.

- Be willing to experiment. Trial and error is the best way to find what works and develop it into what you need to continue to grow.

- Plan a small number of tasks instead of overloading your routine with too many things to do.

- Make sure your routine is aligned with your SMART goals, so you are sure your tasks correspond with what you're after.

- Don't make a big deal if you break the routine or habit. Accept yourself as a human, grow every day, and start over tomorrow.

What you need in your daily routine

Creating your routine can take a lot of time and energy, so it is essential to have specific points that will make your routine successful and fulfilling.

Daily Routine

- Early start

- Time to work out and exercise

- Meditation

- Eating times

- Work blocks

- Self-growth moments

- Hobbies and personal activities

- No screen time

1. An early start

How we manage our sleep time greatly impacts our health and quality of life. Many theories are floating around about which is better, being a night owl or an early bird. Part is this is figuring out which times we are most awake and productive. For example, my brain works best in the morning, it's when I can really focus and tackle my most difficult tasks. However, I don't naturally wake up early! So in order to reach my goals, I set an alarm and make sure the early morning sun comes into my bedroom, to help me wake up naturally too.

Different things determine your energy levels throughout the day, but usually most people are very energetic in the morning. By waking up early, you can take advantage of the most energetic hours of your day. This is also an ideal time for working out. You not only have the energy your muscles need to function at their best but your bodies are stimulated, allowing you to start the day with a clear mind.

Furthermore, starting your day early allows you to approach your day with some reflection (introspection) and planning. Setting aside a few minutes each morning to connect with yourself is important so you can create a realistic schedule based on how you feel and what you consider most important. Lastly, your sleep will benefit from following the natural circadian rhythm. Changing your habits might be hard, yet not impossible if you currently live more at night than early in the morning. It makes sense that you plan your activities in accordance with the cycle of light and darkness.

Light has an enormous impact on our circadian system. So if you wish to be a morning person, try reducing the light exposure at night and increasing it in the morning. This includes electronic devices such as tablets, computers, and cellphones.

Other cues, such as a consistent bedtime routine, can impact your circadian system. We do it with kids and babies, don't we? Baths, teeth brushing, and bedtime stories are all cues for them to understand that bedtime is getting closer. You can probably achieve a similar effect if you make yourself some tea or diffuse some oils before bed, even if you don't have somebody reading you a story or singing you a song.

As with other habits, you've got to be consistent in changing your sleeping patterns: "Start slowly, over a couple of days or weeks, and then keep at it until it sticks." It takes discipline but can be done.

2. A skincare routine

To get started with a skincare routine, there are many things you can do. As with anything, starting slowly is advisable if you've never applied products before. Here are the basics you can follow.

Cleansing

Ideally we should wash their faces every day! Sweat and sebum are produced during the day. It is not disgusting; it is necessary since an unprotected area of the face gets covered. But the skin is oily, so pollution, smoke, heavy metals, dust, and smog adhere to it.

Cleaning your face can be done in various ways, depending on your needs.

Cleaning oil: This is a staple of Korean skincare. A face oil (specially made for the face) is applied to the face and massaged gently to melt makeup and sunscreen. This oil does not adhere to the skin. Due to their formula, they emulsify upon contact with water, making them very easy to remove. You can find lots of different cleansing brands in your local drugstore or chemist.

Soap: You can use it every morning and night. It will remove makeup or sunscreen. If you find it harsh, consider a cleansing gel or balm.

In the evening, use micellar water or cleansing oil to remove your makeup, sunscreen, and dirt from the day. Ideally it's good to wash your face in the morning and evening.

Hydration/moisturizing

Hydration or moisturizing should be the second step in your skincare routine. How are they different? The first provides water to your skin, and the second provides oil to your skin. For a basic routine, let's begin with a moisturizer.

Which should I use? Just as with your other products, it depends on your skin type. Some moisturizing creams are designed for younger skin which may be more oily and prone to breakouts. Others are designed for dryer skin which has lost some of its elasticity. Always choose hypoallergenic products if you have sensitive skin.

Sun protection

All of us should wear sunscreen every day of our lives. No matter what the weather is like, where we are, even if it rains. Unlike other radiation, UV rays are powerful and can pass through walls, glass, and clouds. As a result, sunscreen is more than just a beach necessity.

And what are we protecting ourselves from? It's mainly from radiation that, in the long run, can cause skin cancer. Furthermore, we can prevent spots, wrinkles, and skin texture.

Perhaps you are under the impression that sunscreens are uncomfortable, greasy, heavy, and have white effects on the skin. Thanks to the hundreds of products on the market today, there is something for everyone, including sunscreens with a light texture, mattifiers, and some with colors. There is no reason for you not to protect your skin from the sun.

A correct skincare routine can be summarized in those steps. This may be a good place to begin if you have never used products on your face. Cleanse, hydrate, and use sunscreen in that order. You can apply makeup afterward. If not, you are well prepared to face the adversities of climate change and pollution, with your skin protected.

You can add other products like specific serums or oils as your routine evolves.

3. Time to work out

Experts recommend a minimum of 60 minutes of exercise every day. Considering how much time we spend sitting in front of computers each day, an hour is often not enough to compensate for our sedentary lifestyle's effects.

Exercise benefits all of your body's systems. Dopamine and other neurotransmitters will be released, giving you a sense of well-being throughout the day. Your mental health will improve, you'll have more clarity, and sleep better.

You can activate your digestive system by engaging in physical activity.

By satisfying that need with healthier food, you'll be able to get the most out of your workouts and trigger a cycle of well-being. You can also prevent gaining weight, heart disease, type 2 diabetes, and high blood pressure with regular exercise. Running or lifting weights can help strengthen your bones. Tennis is also a great way to stay fit and meet new people.

Also, it is good to include short workout blocks in your mornings. Training your strength, flexibility, or aerobics skills can take only 20 minutes of your morning, giving your body all the benefits previously detailed.

The most important thing about working out is to enjoy it. Those who find an activity they enjoy will stay consistent with it. In addition to the morning workout, you should try to incorporate it into your daily routine and make it a priority to find an activity you enjoy.

4. Meditation

John Lennon said it best: "Life is what happens to you while you're busy making other plans." Take a second to process this quote. Re-read it if necessary. What comes up inside of you? Is your mind where your feet are, or is it somewhere else?

It's just a moment that makes the difference: the moment we are there, registering what is happening in our lives, whatever it is. If we get distracted, the experience slips away. We could modernize John Lennon's quote: "Life's what happens to you while you're taking out your phone to take a picture."

The first lesson about mindfulness is that it's not about new experiences but new perspectives. True well-being comes from connecting directly with the source of that feeling, inside or outside ourselves. A mindful life is a happy life. And meditation can be a good way to exercise our mindfulness skills daily.

When we cannot find an answer to our problems, meditation offers another way. While meditating isn't a cure-all that will make the pain go away, it provides other benefits. For some, it can produce a sense of peace and determination. You can deepen your understanding through a flash of insight while meditating.

Here are some tips for incorporating it into your daily routine:

1. *What should you wear?*

Start by removing your shoes and getting into some loose garments. Let go of whatever tight clothing or loud accessories you are wearing and get into the meditation mood free of anything that can make the experience uncomfortable.

2. *Where should you do it?*

Meditation should be done somewhere you can feel comfortable and focus on the practice without getting distracted by stimuli from your surroundings. Your house, the park, your garden, the beach, anywhere can be a good spot if you feel it will allow you to slow down and connect with the present.

3. *How should you sit?*

Keep in mind that even if you dedicate a few minutes to it, if you maintain a bad posture to meditate, you will immediately feel discomfort from having your back loaded, your legs numb, or your arms flexed inappropriately, and this will distract you. Whether sitting on the floor or on a chair, keep your back straight but without tension, breathe deeply, and keep your shoulders and arms relaxed.

4. *What happens if thoughts interrupt you?*

When you meditate, different thoughts might arise, personal problems, discomfort at the time, or doubt about whether you are doing it right (which usually occurs when you first start). Accepting these thoughts is important.

Through meditation, we explore the idea that psychological well-being begins with accepting thoughts, emotions, and bodily sensations that simply cannot be changed or eliminated. If you have thoughts like this, accept them and return your attention to the object, breath, sound, or sensation.

5. *For how long should you meditate?*

As you begin to meditate, you should increase the time little by little. To improve your health and well-being, starting with a one-minute meditation is ideal and gradually progressing to 20 or 30 minutes of meditation daily.

Remember that meditation and relaxation should be a pleasant part of your day. Doing it with someone you love or in a place you enjoy will make it a worthwhile moment for you.

5. Time for food

The time we allot to food should be divided into two parts; time for cooking and time for eating. As for the first, cooking, the best alternative is to plan weekly and cook in batches. If you want to eat breakfast at the beginning of your day, schedule a time. Having breakfast before starting your day's work is the best way to get your day off to a good start.

At lunch and dinner, eat mindfully, plan your activities so that they don't interfere with these times, and try not to eat while you work or watch television. Being mindful of our diet allows us to make appropriate food choices. Our metabolism is an important reason we should eat at certain times each day. Nutrition and food experts believe humans must have a body clock that dictates what times to eat to avoid metabolic disorders and nutritional imbalances.

6. Work blocks

How often have you found yourself juggling many deadlines simultaneously in your job? Despite the pressure of being overworked and overburdened, there is a way to remain efficient. This is called time blocking.

Organizing time this way entails categorizing it into differentiating thematic blocks. This way, you know exactly what you must do during each work hour. Additionally, these thematic blocks allow you to structure tasks around a common thread without jumping from one activity to another. This saves us time and keeps us focused. Knowing a specific time is dedicated to a task, and nothing else, allows your mind to focus on what you are doing, which will free up your ability to think and create.

Organizing your work this way allows you to have a daily action plan, which will prevent you from missing deadlines for tasks that become urgent.

The most important aspect of structuring your work time in blocks is determining how much time is required for an action to be effective. In other words, determine how long each task will take. Otherwise, if you schedule your time unrealistically, you may experience the stress and frustration of having set yourself an impossible pace.

7. Self-growth moments

Similar to sports and meditation, self-growth will not happen without some time devoted to it in our schedule. To incorporate it into your daily routine, you must understand that it consists of two distinct components: unlearning and incorporating new ideas.

Unlearning means putting aside part of those models that inhabit our environments and that we have internalized to create something new. To do so, we need self-awareness and critical thinking skills, which we train when meditating.

And that's when incorporating new ideas comes into the picture.

By reading or listening to podcasts daily, your knowledge level will continue to grow and grow as you become more aware of new topics. You will learn new vocabulary, improve your spelling, and you will also be able to learn new things with each book, such as culture and history. The more we read, the more we discover.

Just by reading 20 minutes a day, you will see the difference. It does not have to be 20 minutes straight, it can be 10 minutes during the day and 10 minutes at night. This is approximately 20 pages per day, and although it may not seem like much, if you read 20 pages every day, you will have gotten to 140 pages in a month, you will have read more than 500 pages, and in a year 7000 pages. The average of books is approximately 300 pages; if you don't want to, you can read 25 books in a year. All you have to do is remain constant and dedicated to your personal development.

8. Hobbies and personal activities

Devoting time to yourself as a part of your daily routine might be the last thing you think of. However, you do need time to yourself in order to be able to thrive.

First of all, remember that you need to dedicate a few hours a day to pamper yourself. That can include reading, kickboxing, or any other hobby you choose. Thus, one of the main rules when it comes to hobbies is to realize that they are activities you enjoy and can use to feel motivated or happy throughout your day.

If you allow your free time to be used only to be productive, you'll feel unmotivated and stressed. As a society, we have adopted the idea that we need to be constantly productive or else we are wasting time. It's impossible to be productive every minute of the day, so resting or just doing stuff to relax shouldn't be something we feel guilty about.

9. Evenings off screen

As we're already aware, our body has its internal clock, which is controlled by hormones. When it gets darker, melatonin, a hormone that is naturally produced at night, begins to take over as the day's cortisol production slows down. Hormones like these let your body know it's time for bed.

Screens, such as smartphones, laptops, and TVs, emit blue light, which blocks the "sleepy" signals sent to your brain by melatonin. No wonder you don't have a good night's sleep when exposed to blue light at night.

Turning off screens before bed might be hard, but giving your mind and body a rest period without technology distractions is the goal. To achieve this, try to create a bedtime routine free of screens from start to finish, at least 30 minutes in length. As part of a healthy bedtime routine, the National Sleep Foundation recommends putting electronics away one hour before bedtime.

Devoting some time before you go to bed to prepare for the next day is an excellent way to stay conscious of your routine and daily activities. Set the clothes, put the kitchen in order, and take a moment to go through your schedule.

Finally, it's a good idea to take some time to reflect on your day before you go to sleep. Especially if you can capture your thoughts in writing. This way, you can refer the notes back to track changes over time and tweak your routine based on the real needs you observe.

Always leave room for growth and change

When constructing your routine, you must always ensure there is room for improvement and adaptation. Having a routine has great benefits, and you should take advantage of it. You may observe changes in your personal life, physical and mental health, and the pursuit of your goals.

But be open to the reality that things may need to be adjusted. The next time you notice something isn't working, hit the pause button, and ask yourself why. Don't be afraid of pausing, reassessing, and trying again. To achieve your goals, you must spend time thinking and incorporating them into your daily activities. This way you can reach your goals, be happy and create a life you love.

4. Relationships

Growing up brings many changes to our relationships. We meet new people as we enter new environments, such as the workplace. Friendships that were very close in our adolescence might lose strength. To feel fulfilled and build the relationships we want as we mature, we need some ideas about how to move in each area.

Love

As a general rule, adult relationships tend to be more satisfying than those during youth. As we mature, we enjoy greater emotional balance and well-being. As a matter of fact, experts say that the security and serenity that adult love provides can improve psychological and emotional health.

Mature love is beneficial because it has been worked on individually and as a couple. The intensity of our emotions separates a bond of this type from an adolescent one. Adolescents give themselves over and over again and lose perspective. As adults, we can respect each other's space and work together as a team.

The definition of an intimate relationship is two equal mature people who love each other, work together, share what they have in common, and respect what makes them different. It's a relationship built on interdependence, where they rely on each other equally, without it being a constraint. Each partner respects the other's individuality and accepts the other's behavior. Our differences in interests, values, or concerns will not be attributed to the absence of love or distance but rather to our individual differences.

When thinking about building personal relationships, we need to take into account the following principles:

- *Demarcation:* when two people form a voluntary relationship, they assume the relationship has priority over everybody else (friends, family, work). The couple is voluntary. The decision is made with the aim of having a positive and satisfying relationship between both parties.

- *Priority but not exclusivity:* the couple's relationship will not prevent us from being able to relate to and attend to other people who are important to us

- *Role flexibility:* As a couple, we will face different situations requiring us to adopt complementary roles. We will adjust to one another depending on the situation.

- *Equal value:* the two members of the couple are worth the same. For the simple fact of being alive, each person has intrinsic value.

- *Negotiation:* The ability to resolve conflicts to your satisfaction is a fundamental characteristic of a good relationship. This way, negotiations won't become a power struggle, where we may feel we are losing, but rather we'll be in it for the long haul. We're cooperating, and we're committed. So our willingness to "change" is more positive. To improve our flexibility, we will make changes with which we are comfortable, first and foremost for us. It'll be mutually beneficial in the long run. If a couple has problems, it will have an impact on them both. That's why it's important to look at it from both sides.

By keeping these principles in mind, you will be able to build a strong and valuable relationship and avoid toxic ones.

Work

Most of our adult lives are spent at work, in the organization we dedicate ourselves to. We all know that the quality of our work environment and relationships determine our willingness and motivation to tackle the tasks at hand. Our workplace relationships can also lead to friendships.

The whole organization contributes to the work environment. To improve the environment day after day, human resources managers must do their part, as well as collaborators, middle managers, and the basic workers. In light of this, the following five tips will help you maintain a healthy and valuable work relationship, enabling us to feel satisfied and happy.

- *Fluid communication:*

Good communication helps organizations reach their goals and boost productivity. It's essential for relationships. We should avoid talking about our colleagues and making negative comments behind their backs because that can damage communication and create problems.

When communicating with others, we must always be direct. It's also a good idea to avoid work issues in our free time, since learning how to improve the other aspects of our work relationships is important.

- *Do not blame other people:*

We're often not responsible for mistakes or problems the company as a whole commits because blaming third parties isn't our job. We can deal with this issue without having to accuse other people. Still, we should keep in mind that we're all human, and we all make mistakes, so let's not speak ill of anyone. We can start by assuming our role in the matter and helping the people who need it.

- *Share success:*

We should not feel bad or jealous of our colleagues and friends who succeed in achieving goals or completing a project before us. In fact, quite the opposite is true. We must be happy for others and learn from them to be able to apply their strategies on our own.

If other people's work is sincerely and positively valued, the climate and labor relations will be strengthened. In addition, this will demonstrate the team's great camaraderie and interest in achieving common success and avoiding rivalries or misunderstandings.

- *Positive attitude:*

As repetitive as it sounds, the attitude with which work is handled daily determines the success of all employee relationships. You should not transport personal problems to the workplace.

Your interest in others and friendliness will bring people closer together and improve the environment. The best way to make the day-to-day work in the organization excellent is by being cheerful and generating good conversations with everyone.

- *Help and allow:*

Sometimes you need others' opinions and help. It's then that we realize we have good relationships and how vital they are for a job well done.

We should make ourselves available to help others and let them help us when needed. Teamwork is best if you're looking to achieve goals, improve daily, and create a climate of respect and trust.

Friends

As social beings, we all need friends (there is even a national day to celebrate friends!). Nevertheless, the kinds of friendships we cultivate can change over time. Kids have a remarkable ability to call someone their friend. When they see a child their age at the park, they already consider him their friend, even though maybe they don't even know his name.

With age, this concept changes, and there are more conditions to consider someone a friend. When is someone considered a friend? A friendly relationship depends on two people finding something in common, an affinity, according to the RAE. It could be sharing a hobby, an activity, an experience, or simply having similar interests.

As human beings, however, we cannot remain static all the time. Just like our bodies, our experiences, interests, and priorities will also change in the future; as a result, our friendships will also change. Adapting is necessary in the face of these changes, which can sometimes result in a crisis. There is a pressing need for adjustment to this new situation, leading to two possible outcomes: that our bonds of friendship are maintained and remain through the storm; or that they break.

To maintain a relationship, both sides should have the real desire to do so. Healthy relationships require respect, tolerance, listening, and sincerity. Every friendship has its own level of demand and, therefore, requires its own level of care.

We all live in a world where relationships play a significant role in our everyday lives. As important as working on ourselves and our projects is, working on the bonds we have with the people we love is also important. To have a fulfilling life, we need more than "professional success," we need to share it with people we love.

5. FAQs and hacks

What to put in your first aid kit

The best thing to do in an emergency is to be ready. What should be included in a home first aid kit? Here is a list of some of the most important basic things you should include:

- Alcohol wipes or alcohol gel

- Antiseptics such as hydrogen peroxide and iodized solution.

- Band-aids or bandages of different sizes to cover the wound or control bleeding.

- Sterilized gauzes.

- Physiological serum.

- Sticking plaster.

- Scissors.

- Gloves.

In addition, your first aid kit should be kept in a clean, safe area. And of course, it should be accessible. Reviewing it at least twice a year to replace expired items is a must.

What to do in case of an allergic reaction

The first thing you should do is assess the severity of the allergy. This can be mild, such as an itchy mouth or skin or coughing from dust or pollen. Or it can be severe, such as large hives or patches on the skin or severe difficulty breathing. In the first case, it is ideal to identify what is causing the reaction and avoid contact with that substance. Not eating a certain food, avoiding using a particular cream, or simply closing the windows so that dust does not enter from the outside.

In the second scenario, the situation is complicated, so talk to someone more knowledgeable. The best option is to visit a doctor.

Which contraception method is best for you

To start with, you need to know that a condom is the only method that, in addition to preventing pregnancy, prevents sexually transmitted diseases, so it is very important that you use one.

Women can supplement protection with contraceptive pills that, in addition to preventing pregnancy, can also help you to reduce acne and hirsutism, regulate menstrual cycles, have less painful periods, and manage other conditions associated with menstruation.

Other methods, however, are more complex and require more dedication. Therefore, examining and analyzing them carefully is convenient before deciding on them. Among these are IUDs (Intrauterine Devices) that must be placed by a gynecologist, the diaphragm for women who do not want a hormonal method, or injectable contraceptives or contraceptive patches.

Why should you wear SPF daily?

The use of sunscreen is not limited to summer vacations or trips to the pool since exposure to the sun without protection has the same consequences all year long.

When walking to the supermarket or running in the park, you are less aware of it, which is when it harms you the most. In technical terms, the sun causes skin aging by forming free radicals, which destroy collagen fibers. As a result, wrinkles, sagging, dehydration, and spots can appear. Significantly higher exposures can result in skin cancer.

For all these reasons, starting to use sunscreen every day is a good choice.

How to treat a burn

Your treatment will depend on how severe the burn is. Burns are categorized according to their severity. The first degree is the least serious, affects the outer layer of the skin, and causes little pain, redness, and swelling. The second degree affects deeper layers and causes blisters. Third- and fourth-degree burns may damage joints and bones, which need to be treated in a hospital.

You should first put the affected area under cold water for about 20 minutes. As soon as the burning sensation has diminished, you should gently wash the burnt area with water and soap. At a later point, you can continue adding something cold every five to fifteen minutes, depending on the severity of the pain. For serious burns, you should seek medical attention asap.

CPR basics

When dealing with a person who can't breathe normally or if they are breathing heavily, knowing these steps can be beneficial since you can save their life. The first thing to do is contact an emergency service or request help while doing CPR.

To do the chest compressions, you must first find the center of the chest, placing two fingers at the junction of the ribs and the base of the other hand on top of the two fingers.

While pressing with the base of one hand and the other on top of it with the fingers intertwined, you should do about 100 compressions per minute, that is 1 or 2 per second, as long as the chest drops at least 2 inches (5 cm).

If this does not work, a more complex step must be performed, and you should have prior training for this. It takes 30 compressions followed by two breaths, and you must repeat this cycle as often as necessary until the patient can breathe by themselves.

SMART goals template

Specific: What exactly do I want to do?

_____

_____

_____

_____

_____

Measurable: How will I keep track of my progress?

_____

_____

_____

_____

_____

Attainable: Is this something I'm capable of?

_____

_____

_____

_____

_____

_____

Relevant: What is the purpose of this? Is it important to me?

_____

_____

_____

_____

_____

Time-orientated: When will I complete this?

_____

_____

_____

_____

_____

How to identify friendships that empower you

When choosing friends, it is essential to know how to tell the difference between positive friendships and toxic ones.

Positive friend

- Encourages you to achieve your goals

- Cheers you on

- Shares in your happiness when you succeed

- Treasures your friendship.

- When you're together, you feel good about yourself

- A friend like this makes a positive difference in your life, and you also make a positive difference in his/hers.

Toxic friend

- Secretly sabotages your dreams and success by causing you to doubt.

- Is someone jealous of your relationship and wants to exploit it to manipulate you.

- You feel uncomfortable with him/her and conclude that it must be you.

Part 3: Career & job success

Finding a job

It can be difficult to land your first job, but it is also an important milestone in your professional career. Your first job can change the course of your career. For instance, you might discover activities that you genuinely enjoy, which you end up specializing in, or you might find a job niche that opens doors for you.

You can do a few things to make your job search easier. There are many online job sites you can join, both for jobs in specific areas, and also for work from home jobs. If you are in college, do you have internship opportunities? When starting, this is always a good chance to get into the professional world.

Many jobs today require candidates to go through an internship before being considered for trainee or effective positions. Therefore, if you are still an undergraduate student or in the middle of a professional course, it is recommended to start by finding a great internship opportunity.

Exercise networking: it's time to meet people and activate your contacts

The help of a contact can facilitate your first opportunity in the market. The person can recommend you for available jobs in the company where he works or also highlight your profile to other professionals who have open jobs in their work teams.

Another point to consider when looking for your first job is networking. Seeking connections is important at any point of your career, but especially at the beginning. This is because when you meet interesting professionals, in the beginning, they may become good connections in the future.

You can start by connecting with people who are already close to you. People from your course, professors, or other students are a good option if you are in university or a technical course. Also, finding cheap or free courses related to your professional interest in your city may be a good investment at this point. You will not only grow in knowledge, but if you make the most out of that opportunity, you may find valuable contacts with interesting opportunities for your career.

Lastly, attending free events in your area and approaching people for coffee can help you make friends. A conference, seminar, fair, or congress can be an excellent opportunity to stay up to date and to meet new people.

Choosing the right area, preparing yourself for the interview, and putting together a good CV are all important steps in turning an ideal opportunity into a proposal.

Your resume

Considering that a resume is the first step into the world of work, you'll want to carefully consider the details since it's your chance to make a great first impression. If you are building your first resume, lack of experience can be a major concern. Experience is always valuable, even if it appears small, but you can also include other items on your resume.

What should your resume include

Consider your lack of experience an opportunity to learn and start from the ground up in a company instead of a shortcoming. Focus on the things you have regardless of your experience.

- **Personal information**

Include your full name, city, ID number, social media profiles and cell phone numbers. There is no need to enter your marital status or more information.

- **Photo**

Choosing the right picture for your resume is very important. It should show you as a trustworthy and professional person. This does not mean you should not smile in your pictures; a slight smile will make you look energetic and fresh. In any case, it's best to use an official-looking picture with a suit or shirt, preferably with a plain background.

- **Profile**

Briefly describe yourself as "Who I am", in a formal way that is not technical. Include your last level of education, main interests, career objectives, skills, and why you are a good candidate for a company. Four to five lines should be enough.

- **Education**

From the most recent to the oldest, list the levels of your studies chronologically. In addition, list the courses, workshops, etc., you've taken.

- **Achievements**

Highlight any type of recognition, scholarship, award, research, monitoring, publications, volunteering, group participation, award achievements, or any other situation illustrative of your work and leadership style.

- **Professional experience**

For inexperienced candidates, it is the most feared part of their resumes. It's okay if you don't have work experience yet; just remove this section from your profile and complete the rest. Nevertheless, if you have done an internship, some part-time work (delivery person, waiter, etc.), or any volunteering with an association. Those little experiences prove you're responsible and hardworking. In this case, it is good that you include them in this section.

· **Skills**

Take this opportunity to list all the things you're skilled at, like, technological programs, leadership abilities, public speaking, writing, typing, etc. This is the place to show off. Be sure to note which skills and competencies will make you stand out.

· **Languages**

Companies often like to see you speak more than one language since communication with people from other countries who speak a different language is important in this globalized world.

· **References**

If possible, include one or two references who can speak honestly about your abilities. Many people can verify the information on your resume, such as your teachers, classmates, previous employers (if you had any), and others.

How to draw attention to your resume

Since the people who work in personnel selection are usually quite busy, the visual impression your resume makes is essential. To ensure your resume isn't discarded immediately, follow these tips below to get the employer's attention so that your CV will be reviewed.

- Don't use strong colors or hard-to-read fonts. When you submit your resume to a recruiter, make the first meeting friendly and pleasant. They can concentrate on the content if they do not have to make much effort to understand the style.

- Don't have any spelling mistakes. Your ability to write well is directly related to your education level and your ability to express yourself well, which is required in many different positions within organizations. A situation like this would reflect poorly on you and lead to a deduction in points.

- Whether you are preselected will depend on how and what you say. The key is to captivate your reader with short sentences describing your abilities, skills, and other characteristics valuable to the company you want to work for.

- You must express your ideas dynamically, enthusiastically, and positively. It is important to show that you are open to learning and collaborating. Dynamic and motivated employees will always be important within organizations, so project this.

- Your resume should not exceed two pages. Employers will let you know when they need more information, so do not expand too much in your job descriptions.

Not even the most experienced doctor finds it easy to land a new job since job hunting is also a matter of attitude. We must capture information carefully on our resumes because it will be our first chance to make contact with someone who can offer us the opportunity we are looking for. The second chance to make a good impression is in your interview, so prepare for that too.

The job interview

You made it to the interview stage because your resume stood out from the rest. Yet, you shouldn't be overconfident and miss the chance to show your talent and how well you are suited for the position. A job interview can be successful if you listen carefully to the questions asked by the recruiter so that you avoid making mistakes that might make you look bad.

In a selection process, you will usually go through more than one type of interview, so knowing what to expect is important.

Types of interview

Directed interview

This format is used mainly by human resource professionals; it follows a structured pattern of questions. During the job interview, the interviewer asks questions concisely and notes the candidates' answers, which must also be concrete.

Non-directed interview

Typically, these job interviews are conducted by people who are not human resource professionals; they are characterized by their lack of structure and the opportunity for the applicant to take the initiative. The interviewer listens rather than asks more general questions. Through this format, the personality of the interviewee can be further analyzed.

Mixed interview

Combining the two previous types, this method allows the interviewer to ask specific questions and provide opinions and comments to the interviewee. This type of interview is very common.

Panel Interview

In the panel interview, you will be the only one interviewed by a group of interviewers. The objective is to evaluate from different angles if your incorporation will benefit the company and, if it does, in which role you will fit best.

You should behave as you would in a standard interview, answering each separately while smiling and remaining calm. Try to act as if you are a part of a group of acquaintances.

Group interview

One or more interviewers and several interviewees are present here. This type of interview aims to evaluate the candidate's leadership capabilities, interaction with the group, or other behavioral characteristics.

Telephone or online interview

This type of interview aims to make a preselection before going to the personal interview. While this is less nerve-wracking, the disadvantage is that you don't know who is interviewing you, and you can't use your presence to your advantage.

A job interview can be stressful and nerve-wracking, so being prepared can help control your nerves and increase our chances of success.

· Practice in front of a mirror or with a friend or family member: Doing this before the interview will help you control your non-verbal language during the interview and correct your mistakes. It will also help you organize your ideas and answer the job interview questions more confidently.

· Find out about the company: It is essential to know what it does, what products or services it offers, and its position compared to the competition. You can find out more about the company and how they communicate on their website.

· Dress according to the company environment: If the job is for a bank or consultant, you should wear a suit or formal attire. However, if the job vacancy is at a start-up or a young company, you can dress casually without exceeding the informal boundaries.

· Take a small notebook and a pen: You may need to write down conclusions, questions, or impressions that may arise during the job interview. It is advisable also to bring two or three copies of your resume since you may find yourself with more interviewers than you thought.

· Remember to be punctual on the day of the interview: This is the first step to demonstrating your professionalism and responsibility.

· Control nonverbal language: Avoid playing with objects while interacting with the recruiter, such as pens, and always look him in the eye to demonstrate calm and security.

· Balance your speech: Highlight your abilities, show your desire to learn and work, and avoid bragging or pretending that you already know everything.

· Explain yourself well, answer briefly and coherently: You mustn't interrupt the interviewer and listen carefully to their questions. This will help you answer more accurately.

· Maintain an optimistic, positive and receptive attitude: Ask the recruiter questions at the end of your interview to indicate your interest in the position.

· Do not lie: Recruiters will automatically turn you down if they discover deception or manipulation. Highlight your strengths and qualities only.

Getting a job is not impossible, but it takes commitment and time. Having found the one you're best suited for, it's time to prepare for your first day.

What questions should I expect in my first interview?

"Tell me about yourself."

This type of question is often the first in a job interview. You need to briefly explain who you are (experience, professional profile, training, etc.). The presentation must be brief and focused on the job you desire.

"Why are you looking for a job?"

It would be good to discuss how you need to advance your career or make it complete by gaining experience in other professional fields. If you are unemployed because you were fired, you need to maintain a positive attitude and not dwell on the reasons for the dismissal. Instead, focus on developing a satisfying and interesting career.

"What do you know about us?"

This is probably one of the most common interview questions since you should know about the company before going for an interview.

Getting to know the company is something you should do before you even apply for a job. If not, you will appear uninterested, reducing your chances of getting hired.

"Why do you want to work with us?"

You must prepare an answer that combines your professional development plan with the research you have already done on the company.

"What is of most importance to you in your life?"

You don't have to say that your work is the most important thing to you out of obligation. The best answer would be one that encompasses several aspects of your life. For example: "To me, it's important to strike a balance so that I can enjoy all aspects of life, including spending time with my family and dedicating time to growing professionally."

"What is your experience with the position?"

A perfect profile for the job puts all your points in your favor and shows you are the best candidate. If this is not the case, think about how your experience and technical skills fit into the position in advance.

"What do you like most about the position?"

You must prepare a thoughtful response for these types of questions in a job interview and explain how you are perfect for the position.

"Are you in any other selection process?"

This can be answered honestly. If you are in another selection process, you do not need to mention the company, only the sector and the position you are applying for.

"What would you highlight about yourself as a professional?"

To answer this question in a job interview, you must choose the technical and personal skills you possess that are most relevant to the job. If the position is for a department head, you can highlight your leadership skill, whereas if it's for a technical position, you can emphasize your attention to detail. You should not overlook your qualities as a person, such as honesty, teamwork, responsibility, commitment, and proactivity.

"What is your biggest flaw?"

This is one of the most difficult interview questions to answer. You should pick a minor defect to demonstrate you are aware of it and trying to improve it. Turning a defect into a virtue is already widely seen and may sound false.

"What have you done to broaden your experience?"

Now is the time to demonstrate your proactive approach to your professional development, so please mention any training you have completed related to that goal. Additionally, you may mention personal projects or hobbies that demonstrate qualities such as leadership, organizational skills, etc.

"How are you working in a team?"

It is one of the easiest questions to answer in an interview. Even if you are applying for a position where you work alone, you should emphasize that you enjoy working with others. Use an example to illustrate your point.

"Do you prefer to be feared or liked?"

The question refers to co-workers and employees. Respect might be the right word to use here.

As a professional, I prefer to be respected. In the medium term, fear is not very motivating, so it might not be the best response. Being liked for its own sake is not very productive for a company. Working towards goals and using defined terms is more important.

"What motivation do you need to do a good job?"

These questions in a job interview are common, but avoid mentioning money. Make emphasis on topics like personal satisfaction from problem-solving, improving things, etc.

"When under pressure, how do you cope?"

The key is to be positive in your answer. You may not get the job if you claim that you don't perform well or block yourself.

"What is your greatest professional achievement?"

The best thing is to talk about a project in which you have been involved and has given good results. Do not try to present yourself as the "star" of the project, it is better always to emphasize your participation as part of a work team.

"Tell me about an idea you have had that has been carried out."

If you can provide real facts, you can discuss a change you implemented in your team and how their manner of working allowed you to be more productive.

"What financial aspirations do you have?"

If you want the best answer, you should learn about the salary ranges for that position and about the current situation of the company.

"Where do you see yourself in five years?"

A question like this in a job interview aims to discover how you see yourself developing professionally and if you have a clear vision of where your career will go. You don't need to be very precise since nobody knows what the future holds, but you could discuss how you would like to progress in a particular field or hold positions of more responsibility. Demonstrating a minimum of ambition is the goal.

"What do you do in your free time?"

Use the question to demonstrate how you apply your strengths in your personal life. You play soccer with your friends because you love working together to accomplish a goal. Because you know how to organize a project, you have renovated the house yourself.

"Do you speak any other languages?"

The best way to answer this question well is to do it in the language or languages you mentioned in your resume.

"Why should I hire you and not someone else?"

This is becoming one of the most common questions in recent years, and it is usually asked at the end of a job interview. It's time to remember that your skills, experience, or education fit perfectly with the job description. You can achieve this by making a small list of these favorable points and communicating it to the interviewer. Additionally, remember not to use this question to disqualify the other candidates participating in the selection process, as it could turn against you.

"To finish, do you have any questions?"

When you find out about the company, think of two or three interesting questions you could ask at the end of the job interview. If you have not been answered before (normally, the interviewer introduces the company), choose one and do it at the end of the interview. Even if they don't ask you this question, ask one. It will show your interest in the position.

Small talk recommended topics for the office

Having some topic ideas to share quality time with your co-workers is always a good idea. Some of the best things to talk about are:

- Weekend plans

- Sports

- TV series

- Cooking

- Hobbies in general

- Local news

- Family anecdotes

- Traveling

- Parties, social events, and concerts

- The weather

Stay away from talking about:

- Other people's bodies

- Salary

- Internal critics

- Politics

- Religion

- Gender beliefs

- Personal problems

Going to work

Feeling nervous or anxious is normal when faced with so many new things like new colleagues, bosses, plenty of information, and a new environment that functions differently from your former one. You can have an excellent first day at a new job if you're prepared and consider a few simple things.

Arrive early

It is essential to arrive on time on the first day at work, but it is also a good idea to arrive early. If possible, try to arrive fifteen minutes before your appointment. Plan and use a map app to find the best routes from home to work.

You will not have to study route options if you have a remote job. Still, you will have to get up early, shower, pick an appropriate location (with good lighting and background you will not be ashamed of), and connect punctually or a few seconds before your meeting time.

Ask questions

You will have many questions on your first day at work since you will receive so much information.

Don't hesitate to ask what has not been resolved about your role and obligations, the company, the processes, or the tools you'll be using. It's not a sign of weakness or ignorance but interest.

Get organized

Organizing begins before you leave home and continues once you reach work. Be sure you have all the essentials on hand (computer, pen, notebook, sheets or tablet to record your notes, your glasses, a bottle of water, etc.) and prepare your work area so that your first day on the job is more comfortable and enjoyable.

Relax and enjoy

It is common for a job to create anxiety, especially in environments that have a culture of perfectionism and competition, where results are emphasized. A similar or greater degree of this can also happen on the first day at work.

Be prepared for that anxiety or nerves of starting a new job by getting enough sleep the day before (between seven and eight hours) and giving yourself time to make it to work or the video call.

Relaxation and breathing techniques can also help you feel better if needed.

Your body language

Having the right attitude and body language can help you to present yourself as a person who is open, pleasant, and trustworthy on your first day of work.

For this, you should sit upright, avoid turning your back, look at your conversation partner, and smile when appropriate.

If they invite you to eat, accept

In your first job, the details are important, and mealtime is no exception. You might have brought a salad or some macaroni in a Tupperware or planned to eat at home or your favorite restaurant.

If your colleagues or supervisors ask you to join them for lunch, go along: it is an excellent way to get to know the company, the environment, the relationships, and the people you will live with in a less formal setting.

Learn the language of the organization

All of you will speak one language (or more, if it is a multilingual environment), but each company will also speak its own language. This one is filled with colloquial expressions, abbreviations, acronyms, acronyms, winks, and other elements that can confuse an outsider.

Do not be afraid to ask about them, and try remembering them all (you can write them down). This will make your understanding of meetings and emails and subsequent adaptation easier.

Find out what the professional expectations are

Knowing what is expected of you and your new role will enable you to meet expectations and, if possible, exceed them. On the first day, ask your supervisor about your responsibilities, take notes, and ensure you understand the job's standards.

Turn off your cell phone

Turn off or silence your mobile phone until you need it. Your first day of work can be filled with news, information, presentations, and learning, and you'll need all the concentration you can muster.

Start building your network of contacts

With luck, this will only be the first of many first days at work. Your relationship with your colleagues may be key to your adaptation, resolving doubts, especially in the first weeks, and even developing friendships.

Say thanks

"Rookies" need to be grateful. Thanking those who helped you on the first day of work (and for the opportunity to be a member of the team and company) demonstrates education and respect. This will also prove your positivity and willingness to contribute to the company.

Clothes

To begin with, there is no set rule for what constitutes a professional look since the work environment determines the code of style. You should consider the image of the company, the size, the average age of your colleagues, and the role you play. The style of the interviewers you saw during the selection process can be useful as a guide.

Casual

You can dress casually if you work in an informal environment without direct contact with clients. Sometimes even companies with formal dress codes offer casual Fridays so that you can be comfortable and sporty. However, a casual office appearance does not mean sloppy, or looking like you don't' care about the job. Stay away from slippery dresses, shorts, and tops with spaghetti straps. You can wear sneakers with jeans in this style. Just not ripped jeans.

Smart Casual

This look is trendy in young companies with young employees and a professional attitude. The basis for this style is blazers and shirts without ties, pastel-colored blouses and palazzo or cigarette pants, and knee-length dresses. Sporty looks and more elegant elements combine in the smart casual dress code. All in all, it's a professional yet comfortable outfit that will make you appear friendly without losing credibility.

Business casual

As it stands, this dress code has a formal office look. In addition to professionalism, comfort and accessories also play a part. It's the ideal look for structured businesses, especially for meetings or lunches with clients. A suit is appropriate for men, but women can choose soft or straight-cut skirts or trousers in the version without a tie. Pastel shades and soft colors are perfect.

Business

This is the most important part of any office wardrobe. Even if you are not part of a large corporation, consider it the best choice for conferences, meetings, and presentations. Jacket and tie for him, blue, gray or beige, suit jacket and pants or jacket for her. Closed shoes, heels, but not more than 10 cm.

How to get a promotion

A career promotion is one of a professional's most important goals. It represents an improvement in your career and offers the chance to keep advancing. As a result, it is recognition for your commitment.

Promotions are an excellent indicator of career growth. Promotion is also highly motivating for any employee since it represents professional advancement and benefits one's quality of life - but only if that is one of your life goals. Promotion signifies recognition of service, loyalty, and professionalism. It is also proof that you are valued by the company you work for. Additionally, it represents the challenge of growing on a personal and professional level to fulfill your new position's responsibilities. You need to know where you are in your career and understand what you lack to reach the next level.

Promotions allow the company to fill specific positions with professionals familiar with them.

Promoting you, a professional with experience and knowledge of the company, its policies, and culture, automatically eliminates the need to select and train new employees.

You can be promoted without changing your position in the organization chart. Changing your role and responsibilities is part of a job-level promotion; however, this doesn't entail moving offices or changing jobs. Instead, it is an adjustment to your job description. Sometimes, you will need to seek internal advice to complete this process. You can find out what promotions are available by contacting Human Resources. Remember that promotions are not always about changing positions.

Which types of promotions are there?

It can be job rotations, transfers, or promotions. All these mean different things, and we usually get confused between these different types of movements. A job rotation may imply a change in your work description without new benefits, while transfers can include experiencing a change of headquarters or department. However, you will continue to perform the same tasks wherever you are assigned.

When it comes to promotions, there are two main types you can aspire to. You can earn a promotion through seniority. This means that promotions are based on years of service. You can also earn a promotion by merit. This means they can be faster to get and will depend on your performance.

How Do I Get a Promotion at Work?

Every company has its own promotions, but there are some common factors that make you a good candidate. It usually starts with a need. Some functions are not covered, so a gap opens up. Internal changes and upcoming projects also lead to these gaps.

Although different scenarios can generate the possibility of promotion, experts in the field of human talent agree that the following qualities define a successful candidate for promotion:

- Productivity: Being able to carry out and promote the company's projects is key. Employees with vision, who are goal-oriented, and take plans to the next level, are the right candidates.

- Leadership: Being a leader means not being afraid to create and execute ideas independently.

- Availability: Promotions involve increased responsibilities and tasks. To accomplish this, you must be an employee with enough time to tackle the challenges.

- Productivity: One of the key points. As long as you represent benefits and growth for the company, you will be eligible for a job promotion.

You can make getting a promotion easier if you consider some factors.

- Stand out: The best way to make yourself eligible for additional responsibilities is to do the ones you have now very well. You'll demonstrate that you're capable and ready for the next step.

· Make sure you are qualified: The most important step is preparing for your desired position. Spend some time studying the position and the new areas. Take courses, learn a language and improve your professional skills.

· Talk to your superior: Discussing your interest in a promotion is a great way to be considered. Make your superiors aware of your desire for more responsibility.

· Observe: This task is simple but crucial. You can become the solution if you recognize the needs of the business.

· Know the methods to get recognised and ear-marked for promotion: To ascend, you must know what to do. Learn what a promotion candidate's profile looks like.

· Find out if you want the promotion: Make sure you want those responsibilities. Understand what the promotion entails before applying for it.

· Make yourself known: Popularity is key because this likable and friendly behavior makes room for leadership.

·   Have a plan: You need to draw up an action plan. Moving forward and knowing what steps you need to take is a must.

When it comes to job promotion, there are no shortcuts. Professional accomplishment results from your time and disposition and, most importantly, from your preparation. You have to be fully trained and dedicated to it. As a result, do not rule out the possibility of training, gaining experience, and growing professionally.

Working from home

There are many benefits of working from home, but it's a lifestyle that requires self-discipline if you want to sustain it into the future. Even if you're glued to the computer all day, you can fool yourself into thinking something is work that isn't. Getting distracted by social media isn't working! By following these steps, you can create a helpful physical and mental environment for being productive.

Establish a routine (or several)

For your body and brain to know when to work and rest, you must maintain a certain amount of regularity in your daily routine. Schedule your day according to your individual needs and include work time, rest time, leisure time, and exercise time. Find a routine and schedule that works for you by experimenting with different options.

Plan your daily schedule

Choosing what to do is the most difficult part. You must know what you will be doing each day.

If possible, spend five minutes before going to bed writing down what you will do the next day. Knowing what you will do the next day before you go to bed will help you sleep better and wake up with clear ideas.

The process of planning each day is, of course, based on your weekly review of your projects and tasks. You will need to take a broader view of your goals and responsibilities every few months.

Work on your TMIs first

You must identify the Most Important Tasks(TMIs) when defining your daily action plan, that is, those tasks you must complete as soon as possible since they will bring you closer to completing projects and achieving goals.

Avoid distractions

Every day, you should set aside a few moments to handle email, phone calls, access social networks, read blogs, etc. Then turn them off, and disable your notifications to stop you being distracted while you're working.

You can go a step; further and take the apps of your phone too. There are some software programs you can install on your computer that will also track the time you spend on websites.

Remember why you do what you do

With time, you will likely lose perspective and motivation to keep working hard. Motivating yourself is vital. You can use sticky notes, posters, and reminders to help you remember your values and goals at work. Keep a visual system that reminds you daily why you do what you do, where you are, and where you want to go.

Locate alternative workplaces

As you probably already know, working at home every day is exhausting. Even if your workplace is comfortable, sitting in the same place all day can become tiresome, especially if you do not interact with others. If you're going to a cafe, look for one with WiFi, good coffee, friendly people, and little noise. You can talk to someone about anything and do tasks that don't require as much concentration there; you'll find it refreshing.

Prepare a comfortable workspace

You should reserve an area where you work exclusively and not use other parts of the house for work, like the bed or the couch in front of the TV. Create clear boundaries between work and personal life.

Maintain a clean and tidy work surface where you can easily work. Make sure your workspace is pleasant. You'll spend many hours there, so make sure you get a comfortable chair that allows you to maintain good posture.

Make sure the room is well acclimatized. Don't hesitate; excessive heat or cold will make your workday miserable. Lighting is also crucial. Consider working in a place with good natural light, avoid reflections on the computer screen, and use a cold white light lamp (it won't generate heat) if you work at night.

Having a culture of workplace wellness (in our home offices or regular offices) will allow us to integrate health into our daily routine. Having a clear mind, preventing illness, coming up with better ideas, being more efficient, and dealing with work situations more effectively are some of the changes we will see.

Home office basics

The ten essential elements that your "home office" should have.

1) Computer

A laptop is a good idea if your work requires you to travel frequently. However, getting a desktop computer might make more sense if you don't need to move. Desktop computers can be built to be faster and more powerful than laptops.

2) Internet connection

You need to be connected to the internet. For better performance, a broadband connection is recommended. The signal must be stable and strong, so you can do your work without difficulty. Be sure to hire a reputable service provider.

3) Peripherals

The list includes; a monitor, keyboard, mouse, printer, scanner, webcam, and headphones. A widescreen monitor is extremely important (you can even have two monitors, depending on your work).

4) Phone / Smartphone

You will find it very useful to always have your smartphone and landline when you work from home. Often overlooked, this is no small detail. Keep in mind that they complement VoIP tools.

5) Furniture

You will need a desk, a chair, even a cabinet or shelf for filing documents, books, or other items. They should be functional and adaptable to your needs. It is important to have an ergonomic desk and chair for good posture during working hours. In addition, modern design has led to furniture that appears like "household furniture" that is very comfortable, useful, and functional. If you look carefully, you can design a home that looks like a warm and inviting office while simultaneously being functional for you to work at your own pace.

6) Good lighting

The lighting in your office should be perfect, if possible, natural. You can prevent headaches, eyestrain, and even poor posture due to not being able to see the screen clearly.

7) Memos / Notepads

Whatever your specialty, memos, and notebooks are useful for putting together lists or outlines, downloading ideas, and more. Various materials and designs are available to suit all tastes and are essential for a home office.

8) Software

Instant messaging, email, voice-over IP applications, and automatic backup programs are also helpful. You can also use the online resources to edit documents, share files, manage projects, and do thousands of other things.

9) Office supplies

The supplies include clips, staplers, highlighters, folders, files, scissors, and envelopes. Create a list of everything you need daily and what else you might need. Basic office supplies are an excellent idea to keep on hand.

10) Your personal touch

You need to make your home office "your real home office". Put a picture of where you want to go on vacation, a desk clock, a mini-poster of your favorite doll, etc. It should reflect your style. Have you given it any thought?

Part 4: Entrepreneurship & money

Money management

Financial stability is very important as we develop into adults. This is true if you are a student, an employee, or want to become an entrepreneur. In an economy as unpredictable as today's, knowing how to manage the money we have right now is of utmost importance. Even though we know it is not easy to plan expenses and save enough to build wealth, especially for those who want to start their own business.

Money in our everyday life assumes different forms: credits, taxes, debt, investments, and assets. But before we go into the different areas of your financial world, let's review some basic things to keep in mind when managing money.

The basics of managing money

Write down your fixed expenses

Keeping track of fixed expenses is essential to determine how much income is left over to invest, save or allocate to rest and leisure each month. You must also be aware of the fixed expenses of your business, such as rent and production costs.

Set aside at least 10% of your income

Make sure to reserve at least 10% of your income for investing before paying fixed expenses. This is not just about saving money until you can spend it on something extra. It's also about applying those savings so that they will earn interest and become a significant asset in the future.

Pay off your debts as soon as possible.

As soon as you have received a loan in your name, you may want to consider paying more installments simultaneously to reduce the length of the contract and, of course, interest. If you have multiple loans or credit card debit, pay off the loan with the highest interest rate first.

Learn to invest

You can protect your money by investing, so you don't waste it on unnecessary things. But when we use the word "investment". An investment can be buying some stock in the S&P 500, or it can be buying an online course to increase your knowledge and skills, so you have the tools to generate more income for yourself in the future.

About 10 years ago I invested $1997 in an online course to teach me how to start a mobile app business, without needing to have any mobile app programming skills. That investment paid itself back in revenue many times over.

In most cases, clothes and shoes, luxury holidays and parties are not an investment. We've all read the story of successful athletes or lottery prize winners who blow through millions of dollars over a few months or years, without investing in anything, and end up penniless.

Set limits on variable expenses

Anything that is not a fixed expense is a variable expense.

In other words, an expense can, in principle, be postponed. Nevertheless, in practice, people do not want to stop depriving themselves of small pleasures, like going out with friends, going on a trip, or buying a gift that is not indispensable.

The best thing you can do in these cases is to set a limit. Make sure you set aside a small amount of money for your leisure activities.

Use financial management tools

Several financial management programs and applications are available if you aren't comfortable working with spreadsheets and need a simpler way of controlling your expenses.

They may allow you to upload receipts of credit card payments, track bank transactions, and even insert bill payment reminders. As a result, you are in control of everything that enters and leaves your account. Late fees and interest will no longer surprise you. Try out a few popular apps on the app store.

Look for alternative sources of income

These days, you can earn money by doing many different things from the comfort of your own home. Most of these alternative sources of income only require a computer, internet, and some time. From freelancing to entrepreneurship, there are a ton of options out there for people who want to earn passive income or add extra revenue to their monthly income.

Define an average budget

To avoid unpleasant surprises, take an average of your income from the past few months and identify the periods when you earn more or less, as well as the impact of seasonality on your sales, such as holiday periods, high season, and low season.

You should be able to pay your fixed expenses with your minimum income. In the months of high billing, when you earn more than the average for the year, invest or save your surplus so that you are prepared for the months of low billing.

Buy smartly

Previously, it was explained that how you spend your money impacts your economic well-being.

You can improve your financial reality by joining reward programs, comparing prices on the internet, and buying second-hand products.

Create an emergency fund

Many people spend most of their income, so their financial situation is fragile when an emergency occurs. Aside from your 10% reserve of income for investing, it is important to reserve an additional percentage in case of emergencies.

There is a difference between this fund and the previous one since money in this fund must be liquid and easy to move. On the other hand, investments do not have these characteristics, which is why it is important to distinguish the investment fund from the emergency fund.

The amount of this fund is usually less than the investment fund, but you must also consider it since it can help you make sure you are prepared for anything. In terms of money management, saving and controlling money is only one part. The other is to become more efficient by generating it.

In the end, investing more means earning more, which means more money to buy something important or improve your business.

Investing

Fear is usually one of the common denominators many savers have when deciding to make their money grow. The fear of losing what has been gained is always there. For this reason, it is challenging to invest for the first time. Investments need to be after a lot of thought and research. However, there are a few tips to keep in mind when investing for the first time.

Set an amount to invest initially

The first thing that should be done is to determine what assets you have available for investment. To attain this goal, experts always recommend dedicating to the investment world the income you don't need to live (which does not go to your emergency fund).

Set investment goals

Once you consider your risk profile and the money you want to invest, you can set investment goals. Where do you want to go? What are the goals you have set for yourself? Usually, these investment objectives tend to have a lot to do with the savings we want to generate for retirement, with the goal of maintaining our purchasing power.

The importance of diversification

Regardless of your profile as an investor, it is always important to diversify among the assets to invest. It is known as "not putting all your eggs in the same basket, but different ones". Thus, the possibility that a specific asset's bad behavior harms your portfolio's performance is prevented.

Assets vs. liability

In financial language, there are many specialized terms that, to the general public less familiar with such matters, may present serious challenges when trying to understand the concepts they refer to. A good example is how poorly we usually understand the difference between "assets" and "liabilities". An asset can be viewed in a very elementary manner as a product or good that generates income for its owner. On the other hand, a liability is anything that causes us expense.

Holding dividend generating shares of a company is an good example of an asset since the shares generate income, often through quarterly, semi-annual or annual dividends. It's also accumulating possible revaluations in the share price.

One of the most well-known liabilities is buying a car. Almost everyone makes a car purchase at least once during their lifetime. And, of course, there is a saying that says, "You lose money the second you leave the dealership". This is a genuine truth since the expenses it produces, and its depreciation increases with its age.

However, in the world of financial markets and investments, nothing is black or white. The future market circumstances that determine whether or not you made the right decision. That's why it is important to remember that if the investment you are going to make "keeps you awake at night", don't do it. And always seek professional advice before investing.

Entrepreneurship

Entrepreneurship and starting your own business is very different from managing or working for a company. As an entrepreneur, your goal is to take the initiative and make a decision to pursue a business venture that allows you to enter the market, either by manufacturing a product or by providing a service.

The best way I've seen entrepreneurs succeed is to follow the market. Research what people are already buying and make a better version of it. And there is a very accessible way to figure this out. It's called the internet. Many of us now work online - in addition to our traditional jobs - because the web has changed the nature of work. Through online business, there are an unlimited number of ways to earn income, whether passive or active.

Passive income differs from active income mainly by whether or not you need to be involved when the income is generated. For example, I wrote this book once. But it has bene sold many times.

Once you create the asset, you don't have to do a lot extra to generate revenue from it. Your money increases passively. However, if you're a freelance web designer, then you need to turn on your computer and make new websites every day to get paid.

Online side hustles

You can generate passive income online in many ways. By creating something (a blog, an e-book, online course, print on demand t-shirts, subscription service, mobile apps, a clothing line or an online store), you can generate passive income even when you are not working.

Create an online course

Selling online courses is among the best ways to earn passive income. There are a number of course hosting platforms out there who will host all your videos, payments and student management for a very small fee. Your main responsibilities are to create an online course that people are interested in and would buy, and then secondly, let people know the course exists by sharing tips and fun videos about it on social media - which could be anything from Facebook and Instagram to Tiktok and Youtube.

Online course prices can range in value from $1 to $2000 and beyond! If you add coaching to your courses, you can charge up to $25,000 per person per year depending on your niche and experience.

Sell physical products online

Many digital nomads are entrepreneurs who travel around the world and make money from their laptop. It sounds a little crazy but it works as I've done this too. One of the most popular business types for nomads is ecommerce. That's selling physical products (that you never see or touch!) online, usually through websites like Amazon or Shopify. If you pick the right products, this can be very lucrative. You can also do drop-shipping. The idea is that someone buys a product on your website, and you then order the product to be shipped directly from the producer to the customer. You are a sort of online middleman. If either option sounds interesting, I'd suggest you watch some of the many videos on youtube on this topic.

Become a freelancer

Many online businesses these days hire people from all over the world to work from home and help them grow their businesses.

Great at Tiktok? Cool. Offer to help local businesses grow their following and sales on Tiktok. Great at writing copy? You can get hired as an email or sales page copywriter. Love video editing? Get a freelancing job editing videos for virtual summits, promotions or repurposing youtube videos into reels and Tiktiks.

Love social media?

Perfect. Build up your profile on your platform of choice and you could be an influencer, with brands paying you to share their product online. You'll find tons of examples of this on all the social media platforms.

Sell the things you no longer need

Why not take advantage of Marie Kondo's tips for earning passive income? Get rid of items that no longer serve you and sell them to generate more income. You'd be surprised how many people are willing to buy second-hand books, clothes, and kitchen utensils. This is a fun way to tidy up your house and generate some extra income.

Get paid for sponsored posts on social media

More and more businesses are paying social media accounts to promote their products and services through influencer marketing. Whether you're interested in travel, fashion, beauty, home decor, or wacky dog haircuts, there's a niche for you.

As the most known platforms allow you to create fan pages for just about anything, social media sponsored posts are a great way to earn money.

You don't need to start selling something; building an audience is more important. Companies will offer you their products so you can market them or speak well of them (for a commission or a single payment). Also, don't forget to use hashtags to gain more exposure and reach a larger audience.

Create your own blog

You can make passive income online by creating your blog. Through affiliate links, advertising, courses, sponsored posts, products, book deals, and more, blogging has enabled countless bloggers and entrepreneurs to earn passive income.

It indeed takes time to build a successful blog. However, since it's a great way to earn a passive income, it may be worth the effort.

Join affiliate marketing

It's good to know that almost every big brand has an affiliate program. For instance, some brands' affiliate programs pay up to $2,000 per referral. Other online retailers, however, provide referral bonuses of just 10%. Therefore, you must research the best affiliate programs before beginning your career. You can generate affiliate commissions through blogging without spending any money on ads.

Create a print-on-demand store

Taking advantage of today's e-commerce boom can be a great way to make passive income if you are an accomplished designer. You can sell custom graphics on products like clothing, mugs, banners, phone cases, bags, and more with print-on-demand. What's great about this is that you can create your products and build a brand. Amazon has a print on demand t-shirt program called Merch by Amazon. There are other websites there too like Teespring and Printful.

Write an eBook

The ebook has remained a popular content medium since it became all the rage in 2010. If you are a natural writer, you can earn passive income by writing an ebook.

Create an app

Without a doubt, this is one of the most original ideas on how to generate passive income. You can create applications that generate passive income online as a programmer or developer. You can generate assets by charging a fee to people who purchase your app or make your app free and monetize your passive work with ads. The good news is you also don't need to be a programmer. You can outsource the programming work overseas on a platform like Upwork.

Create YouTube videos

YouTube is a great way to generate passive income online. You can make quite a lot with YouTube, from sponsored videos to banner ads. The key to creating a successful YouTube channel is consistently creating content for a few months.

With time, you'll see that all your efforts are worthwhile, and you'll really enjoy passive income.

Passive income offers a large number of benefits over costs. And the most important thing is that it is not necessary to give up your job to earn extra income if you enjoy what you do.

Whether you want to start by writing an e-book, investing in stocks, or creating content to sell on-demand, consider how much time you can spend earning passive income. After that, getting started is the only thing left to do.

Paying taxes

Taxes are something you'll encounter as you become an adult and start earning your own money. Doing your taxes can be a little daunting for someone without prior experience.

What are taxes, and why do we need them?

Every country has public services such as public education, postal services, law enforcement, health care, and we invest in innovation and technology. People and institutions that provide these public services must, of course, be paid. Citizens pay for those services indirectly through taxes. In the USA, these public services are offered at the state and federal levels. Citizens are taxed both at the state and federal levels.

USA taxes

In the simplest terms, most taxes can be divided into three categories: taxes on your earnings, purchases, and assets. You need to know how taxes work and how they are calculated in order to understand them. You must also determine your taxable income, distinguishing between tax deductions and tax credits.

Understanding how taxes work for businesses and investors differently from how they do for everyday taxpayers is vital. As a result of incorporating these concepts, it will be easier for you to understand how to file a tax return and how to put together a tax plan that works for you.

Taxes on what you earn

The US tax system is set up in such a way that everyone pays their fair share of taxes. In other words, based on your income and the amount you receive, you have to pay taxes on a certain percentage. That can't be done by having a tax rate that is the same for everyone; that would not be fair. For example, if someone earns $200,000 a year and pays 30% in taxes, they would still have $140,000 left over, enough to enjoy a nice lifestyle. On the other hand, if someone earns $40,000 and then they have to pay 30% in taxes, then they only have $28,000 left over, which is barely enough to make ends meet.

As a result, instead of having a flat tax rate in the United States that applies to everyone, we have what is known as a progressive tax system, in which you pay higher tax rates as your income increases. This makes the system a little more equitable since it gives people with lower incomes a tax advantage to make a comeback. The tax rates are summarized as tax brackets.

In 2022, as a single taxpayer, you will pay a 10% tax rate on your first $10,275 taxable income, then 12% on your next $10,276 to $41,775 taxable income and so on. And remember, you are taxed progressively. So, for example, if you make $100,000, even though that puts you in the 24% tax bracket, you wouldn't pay a flat 24% tax rate. Instead, you would only be taxed 24% percent on the income you made between $89,076 and $100,000, which in this case means only $10,924 would be taxed at the 24% tax rate, and the rest would be taxed at the other tax rates. These numbers usually change each year, so make sure to check the latest numbers online

·   **Calculating taxes on what you earn.**

The amount of taxes you owe is determined by your taxable income, which is distinct from what you make overall. You can calculate your taxable income by subtracting your tax deductions. By default, all American taxpayers are given a standard deduction. The amount of your standard deduction depends on your filing status, whether you are filing single, married jointly, married separately, or filing head of household. The numbers also change each year, so check the current numbers in your area.

You can calculate your taxes by taking your total income minus all your qualified deductions to determine your taxable income. Once this is done, you will have a tentative tax owed since tax credits must also be accounted for before deciding your final tax owed.

· Tax deductions vs. tax credits

Understanding the differences between the two is important. In the example above, it was demonstrated how tax deductions help reduce taxable income. Tax credits, however, are applied to your tax liability. For example, if you earned $100,000 in income, and then deducted $25,000 from that, you have a $75,000 taxable income, and you may owe $10,000 in taxes. In that case, if they had a tax credit of $3,000, it would be applied to their tax liability, and they would pay only $7,000 in taxes after the credit was applied.

Generally, tax credits provide a stronger benefit than tax deductions, but you shouldn't seek as many deductions or credits as possible; rather, you should know what is available and useful for your particular situation.

· The role of entrepreneurship and real estate

While taxes are a way to pay for government services internally and externally, it seems that citizens simply paying taxes and governments providing services aren't enough to build and sustain a thriving economy.

Certain tax benefits are only available to certain people, such as tax incentives for investors and business owners. This kind of economy has many quality jobs available so that people can earn a living. Also, a thriving economy is one where people have quality and affordable living places. Two types of people are essential to provide these things: entrepreneurs and real estate investors.

The government gives tax breaks to entrepreneurs and real estate investors to encourage job creation and housing. These tax breaks cover travel expenses, entertainment expenses, clothing expenses, vehicle expenses, job tax credits, and so on.

There are two types of earnings for tax purposes, earned and unearned. Earned income is money that you receive from actively working. Wages, salaries, tips, self-employment income, etc., are examples of earned income. In contrast, unearned income is something you receive without actively working. For example, real estate income, interest income, stock dividends, or any other dividend would be examples of this.

The average person pays more taxes on earned income, especially W-2 income, since these are subject to payroll taxes, which include Medicare and Social Security payments, but usually, the employer covers half.

However, if you are self-employed, you are responsible for all payroll taxes, also known as self-employment taxes. Because of this, unearned income is often the best type of income for tax purposes because you don't have to pay payroll taxes or even income taxes on certain types of unearned income, like the sale of assets or qualified dividends.

It takes a lot of time and hard work to get to the stage in life where you can make investments that turn into unearned income, but the sooner you start, the better.

- **How to build an income tax plan.**

A tax planning strategy involves proactively evaluating how to optimize your taxes to give you the desired result, which could be reducing your overall tax liability, aggressively investing in your business, or planning and saving for retirement. To do so successfully, follow these steps.

1. Understand your tax bracket

Tax plans are probably unnecessary if you do not make much money or do not pay much in taxes. If you are, you should understand where you are and how you can save taxes by shifting tax brackets.

2. Understand tax deductions and tax credits

To meet your overall goals, you can even use online calculators to determine what tax deductions and credits you qualify for.

3. Choose your tax strategy

To maximize your tax situation, you can do many things. Examples include maximizing deductions, optimizing your legal entity structure, planning for retirement, and using insurance strategies. Other advanced tax planning strategies such as investing in real estate or oil and gas may also suit your situation. It's important to stick to just one solid strategy, especially if you have little taxable income.

4. Implement your plan

Once you have selected the tax strategies that best meet your goals, you must implement your plan. This means you may need to set up different retirement or health savings accounts. You may also need to start making investments such as investing in real estate or investing in oil, and gas or even budgeting business expenses for the year and so on.

Taxes on What You Buy

When you purchase something in the USA, various taxes are applied. The price you pay will vary depending on many factors, such as the product you buy, the production process, and the state in which you are located.

· Sales Taxes

A sales tax is a consumption tax on retail sales of goods and services. You have likely seen the sales tax printed at the bottom of your store receipts if you live in the U.S. The U.S. is one of the few nations that use traditional retail sales taxes to raise revenue. All U.S. states collect state and local sales taxes except for Alaska, Delaware, Montana, New Hampshire, and Oregon.

Gross Receipts Taxes

In a gross receipts tax (GRT), the amount of the company's gross sales is taxed, whether profitable or not, without deducting any business expenses. GRTs are harmful to startups, which suffer losses in the early years, and businesses with long production chains.

- Value-Added Taxes

Value Added Taxes (VAT) are consumption taxes assessed on the value added during each production stage. Each business along the production chain pays a VAT on the value of the produced good/service at that stage, with the previous VAT paid for the good/service being deductible at each step. The final customer has to pay VAT without deducting the previously paid VAT. This is a tax on final consumption.

- Excise Taxes

In addition to the broad consumption tax, excise taxes are taxes imposed on specific goods or activities, accounting for a relatively small portion of total tax revenue.

Cigarettes, alcohol, soda, gasoline, and betting are examples of excise taxes. Taxes on excise can be used as "sin" taxes to offset harmful side effects or consequences not reflected in the cost of a product.

Taxes on Things You Own (Property Taxes)

Immovable property taxes are primarily levied on land and buildings and are an important source of revenue for U.S. governments. Property taxes account for more than 30 percent of state and local tax collections in the U.S and over 70 percent of local tax collections. Governments need property tax revenue to support public services, such as schools, roads, police and fire departments, and emergency medical services. In addition to residential property taxes on land and structures, known as "real" property taxes, many states also tax "tangible personal property" (TPP), such as vehicles and equipment owned by individuals and businesses. Taxes on tangible personal property tend to be more problematic since they are less stable, neutral, and transparent.

·   Tangible Personal Property (TPP)

Tangible personal property (TPP) includes items that can be moved or touched, such as business equipment, machinery, inventory, furniture, and automobiles. Taxes on TPP account for a small percentage of total state and local tax collections. Their complexity creates high compliance costs. They also favor some industries over others by being nonneutral, distorting investment decisions.

- Estate and Inheritance Taxes

Upon a person's death, both estate and inheritance taxes are imposed. The estate itself pays taxes on estates before assets are distributed to heirs, but the heir pays taxes on inheritance. Both taxes are typically paired with a "gift tax," so they cannot be avoided by transferring property before death.

- Wealth Taxes

Generally, a wealth tax is imposed on an individual's net worth (assets fewer than liabilities) over a certain year's threshold. Under a wealth tax of 5 percent, an individual with wealth above $1 million would have to pay $50,000 in taxes. An individual with a wealth of $2.5 million and a debt of $500,000 would have a net worth of $2 million.

UK taxes

As with any country, the United Kingdom has a fully-integrated Tax System to manage government spending and sustain the country's development.

PAYE tax

The term PAYE refers to pay as you earn. Employees usually pay tax through PAYE. PAYE ensures that amounts owed over a year are collected evenly on each payday. Whenever you receive a salary, your employer deducts Income Tax (IT), Pay Related Social Insurance (PRSI), and Universal Social Charge (USC). Then they send the amount deducted to Revenue. It is possible to reduce the amount of taxes you pay by taking advantage of tax credits, tax reliefs, and exemptions. Scottish citizens must contribute 10% to the Scottish government.

Consumption taxes

The value-added tax (VAT) has different tax rates. There is a standard rate of 20% and a reduced rate of 5%. This number may change each year. These rates apply to certain categories of goods and services and to fuel and energy facilities. Some basic products, such as books, clothing, footwear, and some types of food, have a 0% tax rate.

How do I calculate taxes?

As a general rule, the tax is not due if the salary does not exceed £10,600. This number may change each year.

Withholding claim

You may be able to get a refund of some of the withheld taxes if you stop working before the end of a fiscal year. However, you have up to four years to apply for the money, and to do so, you must fill out one of the following forms: P45, P50, Q60, P85, P800.

Credit score

The term "credit score" in the USA refers to a range of scores from 300 to 850 based on the probability that a person will pay back their debt on time. Because the U.S. economy is based on credit, a person's credit score is one of the most important data. Although there are several types of credit scores, FICO (for Fair Isaac Corporation) is the one most commonly used. The report is from a credit report created by one of the three main credit bureaus, Equifax, Experian, and TransUnion.

How to improve credit score

You can achieve a good credit score by buying on credit and paying off the credit on time.

You can build your credit history by getting a credit card, making small purchases with it, and paying them off in full or leaving a small balance of less than 30% of your monthly credit limit.

Credit cards and loans are the main types of financial products that improve credit scores. Credit history is not affected by debit or prepaid cards, nor the amount of money in a bank account.

Old accounts are much more important to improving your credit rating than recent ones. In addition, keeping the balance on old credit cards below 30% of the credit limit helps increase your FICO score. In light of this, closing or leaving inactive old accounts is not recommended.

If you do not pay a debt on time, going through repossession by a collection agency, bankruptcy, and other financial problems hurt your credit score and stay on your credit record for seven years. If that period has passed, they do not affect the FICO either for or against.

Debt

There are many different reasons why people end up in debt. The path and circumstances that make you feel you have lost control of what you owe can be endless, from medical emergencies leading to thousands of dollars in medical bills to spending your way into debt. In either case, you must decide to cancel your debts.

Getting out of debt and staying out of debt requires a plan. As long as we follow some guidelines, we can prepare for the worst while hoping for the best. Structure and plans help us keep moving in the right direction. If you lose track of where you are going, a plan will help you get back on track.

While in college, some students may be nervous about borrowing student loans for the first time, opting instead to use their credit cards to assist in paying for personal and educational expenses. You might also consider getting into large loans, such as car buying. Although there are differences between these options, all are forms of borrowing. Therefore, when it comes to canceling debt, it is best to know what to prioritize at the point of paying off debt so that you can calculate your financial decisions accordingly.

When canceling debt, you can do it by prioritizing the amount owed or the interest rate. Whatever payoff method you choose, the most important thing is that you are consistent and organized.

By amount owed.

Following this method, you would list your debts, starting with the smallest and working your way up to the biggest debt.

For example:

- Credit Card #1 – $150 (19% Interest)

- Credit Card #2 – $1,000 (17.5 % Interest)

- Vehicle #1 Loan – $7,000 (4.21% Interest)

- Credit Card #3 – $8,800 (17% Interest)

- Credit Card #4 – $14,000 (18% Interest)

- Vehicle #2 Loan – $27,000 (4% Interest)

- Student Loans – $90,000 (7% Interest)

When all your debts are reorganized, you pay the minimum payments except for the smallest payments. It's important to prioritize paying off the lowest debt as soon as possible. After the lowest debt is paid off, move on to the next one until all the debt is paid off.

By interest rate

As far as paying off debt is concerned, this method makes more sense mathematically than any other. It is aimed at paying off debt quickly but requires a lot of discipline. You may find it works best if you are dedicated and focused.

To begin with, list out all your debts in order of interest rate. List your debts, starting with the largest interest rate and going down to the smallest.

Following the previous example:

- Credit Card #1 – $150 (19% Interest)

- Credit Card #4 – $14,000 (18% Interest)

- Credit Card #2 – $1,000 (17.5 % Interest)

- Credit Card #3 – $8,800 (17% Interest)

- Student Loans – $90,000 (7% Interest)

- Vehicle #1 Loan – $7,000 (4.21% Interest)

- Vehicle #2 Loan – $27,000 (4% Interest)

When the debts are listed, it's time to pay the minimum payments on all but the one with the highest interest rate. As with the last method, pay off the highest interest rate debt as quickly as possible. Once you pay off the highest interest rate debt, move on to the next one until you have paid off all the debt.

In addition to being the fastest way to pay off debt, this method reduces the amount of debt added to other loans by eliminating high-interest rates first. Ultimately, this will save you money in the long run. On the other hand, as you don't always see immediate "wins", you need to be focused and committed in order to succeed.

To choose the right system, you need to be honest with yourself. It is best to start with the system based on the amount owed if you are unsure which one would work best for you.

Ultimately, it doesn't matter what method you choose as long as you stick to it. In the end, it wouldn't matter which plan you chose if you quit halfway through. Sticking with it is more important than which plan you follow.

Savings

Now that we have addressed these aspects of your economy, it is time to put some order into your savings decisions. It is necessary to be aware of what you owe and what you own before you can start saving every month. It means you should look at every dollar you earn and spend, including the interest you pay on your credit card balance, monthly bills, taxes, and savings contributions.

Saving money is not just about saving for its own sake; it is also about saving money to achieve one's dreams. There is a big difference.

There is no doubt that one of the best ways to save money is to set a goal that you can achieve. Start by asking yourself what you are saving for. Is it to get married, go on a vacation, or save for retirement? Then you need to calculate roughly how much money you will need and how long it will take you to save that money. It is a good idea to divide objectives into short-term and long-term goals and establish each separately.

Short-term goals (1 to 3 years)

- Emergency fund (have money to support yourself for a few months, just in case)

- Vacations

- Down payment on a new car

Long-term goals (4 years or more)

- Down payment on a house, remodel, or big move

- Quality education for your children

- Retirement contributions

Setting an immediate goal like getting a new smartphone or holiday gifts can prevent you from getting stuck. Reaching smaller savings goals and enjoying the reward you've saved for can give you a psychological boost that makes saving more rewarding and strengthens the habit of saving.

Buying a house

The purchase of a house is a big event in anyone's life. The sense of achievement you get when you own your home can be very satisfying.

However, not everything about purchasing a house is simple, so you should consider your situation carefully. In most cases, buying a house can create some challenges, such as less freedom of movement and quite often a substantial amount of debt, which you need to ensure that you can afford.

Once you decide to purchase a house, these are usually the steps you should take:

1. Adjust your finances: You must know exactly how much money you have saved and how much you can save in the near future

2. Decide your budget: Once you know this number, you can direct your search to more realistic options so that you don't face problems in the future. By keeping this in mind, you can ensure that you are not distracted by properties that may interest you but are out of your reach.

3. Make sure you have a real estate agent: During the process, you'll need to be guided by someone who knows the field.

Research can be done independently, but a professional should be by your side when purchasing. It can either be recommended by your acquaintances or chosen based on your judgment.

4. Determine the type of financing you need: Consider different loan options and programs to determine which one is best for you. Ensure you know all the conditions, costs, fees, taxes, and other charges. The more you investigate all this, the more prepared you will be to face it in an orderly manner.

5. If you don't like debt (like me) consider a different plan. Start a business, generate extra revenue and use that to buy a property. Then rent out that property and generate more revenue. There are some very useful real estate podcasts out there for the more business minded.

6. Keep an open mind: Don't get hung up on your first option. If you are close to a first choice that you liked, the disappointment may be great if it fails to materialize, and you may also miss out on other options you may end up liking more. This attitude will help you face difficulties and setbacks throughout the search and purchase process.

7. Buy when you are sure: It is not a good idea to make a hasty decision, so make sure you have done all the necessary research.

In the United States, buying your first home is easier than you might think, and you don't need to have large savings or a high income. Some of the programs to consider are:

- HomeReady and Home Possible: These are loans with very low initial payment requirements, close to 3% of the price of the house.

- USDA mortgage loan: This allows you to finance 100% of the house's value without making a down payment. It is aimed at houses in rural areas.

- FHA mortgage loans: They are easy to qualify for, as they can be accessed with better credit scores or higher levels of debt.

- Prefabricated and mobile homes: They are one of the affordable homes and, in many cases, can be financed with conventional mortgage programs.

- Mortgage Credit Certificates: With these, you can object to a tax credit corresponding to a percentage of the interest on your mortgage.

- Down payment assistance: These are grants or loans specific for certain "neglected" or "developing" areas in which income level is not considered.

- Personal loans: They can be used to buy a house at a lower price.

These options can serve as starting points to help you determine which one best fits your situation, and then you can dive deeper by consulting a specialist with more knowledge on the subject.

The fact that you know that options may be within your reach and that you understand what they are about is a good start.

How to choose an insurance plan

Health insurance is very important. If you're already 26 years old, you're no longer covered by your parent's plan. You will need to choose the plan that's right for you.

What should I look for?

·   Options: When you compare plans, consider the total costs, including premiums and out-of-pocket costs.

·   Quality care: Access to personalized medical treatment no matter where you are.

·   Discounted rates: You want in-network doctor and hospital options so you can take advantage of discounted rates.

·   Annual checkups and preventive care at no extra cost. Preventive care, like annual exams and checkups, helps keep you healthy.

·   Easy to use tools: Online tools can help you choose plans, find doctors, and predict costs.

· 24/7 service: When in doubt, you'll want to be able to talk to health care experts and access your claims.

What's 401k?

In the USA, this is an employer-sponsored retirement plan that is eligible for employees where they can make salary reduction contributions before or after taxes. The 401k plan allows employees to save and invest part of the income before taxes are deducted.

Employers offering the plan to their employees may elect to match individual contributions to the plan on behalf of their employees. They can also add a profit-sharing feature to the plan. You need to know that taxes are not paid until the money is withdrawn from the account.

Part 5: EXTRAS - What you need to know!

OK we've covered a lot so far! Here are some extra tips to bear in mind as you begin your life as an adult!

What you need to know about your car

In today's world, getting a car and learning to drive it is easy, but the tough part is understanding how it works and maintaining it. Therefore, here are ten things you need to know to drive safely and maintain your car.

1. *Engine oil*

People mistakenly believe that oil burns fuel in the car, but its primary function is to lubricate, cool, and clean the engine. Therefore, three things can happen to your car if you don't have enough oil: thermal degradation, oxidation, and compression heating. This will cause the oil to do the opposite of what it was designed to do, creating more friction, heating the engine, and building up dirt deposits.

2. *Spare tire*

The last thing you want is to change your flat tire and realize that your spare is also flat. The spare tire is not designed to be a decorative item on your car. It is there in case you experience a flat tire. Therefore, always keep a jack and other tools in the trunk of your car for when you need to change the tire. Checking if the spare part is in perfect working order is also a good idea.

How to change a tire

1. Find a safe location

2. Turn on your hazard lights

3. Apply the parking brake

4. Apply wheel wedges

5. Remove the hubcap or wheel cover

6. Loosen the lug nuts

7. Place the jack under the vehicle

8. Raise the vehicle with the jack

9. Unscrew the lug nuts

10. Remove the flat tire

11. Mount the spare tire on the lug bolts

12. Tighten the lug nuts by hand

13. Lower the vehicle and tighten the lug nuts again

14. Lower the vehicle completely

15. Replace the hubcap

16. Stow all equipment

17. Check the pressure in the spare tire

18. Take your flat tire to the garage.

3. *Wiper washer*

Windshield wipers are a necessity that many people tend to overlook. If you want to keep your windshield wipers in better condition, ensure the rubbers are in good shape and the correct size. You should generally replace them every six months, though it's best to check how often your car's manual suggests changing.

4. *Headlights and taillights*

Headlights and taillights dim over time, so it is recommended that you inspect them from time to time. Checking them is a preventive security measure and prevents you from being stopped by the police or a traffic officer. It is generally recommended to change the headlights every year.

5. *General car maintenance*

Regular car maintenance varies depending on the make and model. The best way to know the ideal maintenance plan for your car is to read the owner's manual, as it will give you the ideal service intervals for your car.

6. *Shock absorbers*

Does your car rock from time to time? Can you hear a screeching noise when you brake or go over a bump or pothole? Then your shock absorbers are probably worn out. This is one of the most common issues with older vehicles, so if you drive a car that's a couple of years old, check your shock absorbers.

7. *Air filter*

It is important to change air filters every six months. When engines get dirty, they can get clogged, so they have to work harder, and this can cause an increase in fuel consumption.

8. *Emergency kit*

You never know when your car might break down, and if it does, then you should have an emergency kit on hand:

- A properly inflated spare tire, wheel wrench, and tripod jack

- Jumper cables

- Tool kit and a multipurpose utility tool

- Flashlight and extra batteries

- Reflective triangles and brightly colored cloth to make your vehicle more visible

- Compass

- First aid kit with gauze, tape, bandages, antibiotic ointment, aspirin, a blanket, non-latex gloves, scissors, hydrocortisone, thermometer, tweezers, and instant cold compress

- Nonperishable, high-energy foods, such as unsalted nuts, dried fruits, and hard candy

- Drinking water

- Reflective vest in case you need to walk to get help

- Car charger for your cell phone

- Fire extinguisher

- Duct tape

- Rain poncho

- Additional items for cold weather include a snow brush, shovel, windshield washer fluid, warm clothing, cat litter for traction, and a blanket.

9. *Brakes*

Brakes are a safety feature that you should never overlook. Watch if the steering wheel jerks as you apply the brake pedals when driving. This could affect your car's stability control system and ABS (Anti-lock Braking System).

10. *Get a good mechanic*

And lastly, get a good mechanic. A good, honest, and knowledgeable mechanic is hard to come by, but if you find one, trust him firmly. Ask friends and family for their recommendations. Don't pick the first one you find to give you low rates. Take your time. You are putting the safety and performance of your car in their hands, so make sure they are good at what they are doing.

What you need to know about traveling

Whether you are a frequent or occasional traveler, having some of the following tips in mind can make things a little easier. Although you may find some of these suggestions obvious, you should still consider them.

Airline miles

If you are traveling a long distance and you are not a member of any frequent flyer programs, consider joining one of them. Collecting miles is a great way to get discounts on shopping, hotels, and more offers.

Sometimes these programs, like certain credit cards, give the right to use airport VIP lounges, spaces with exclusive paid or free services, depending on the case.

Beware: cheap can be expensive

Before booking a flight or reserving a hotel, do not get carried away exclusively by the price. Assess the consequences of your decisions. Sometimes the cheap option turns out to be expensive. Due to lack of public transportation, cheap tickets purchased off-peak may force you to take a taxi, pay more for your luggage than anticipated, or spend more on food while traveling. The same can happen to you with a hotel far from the center or a vehicle rental.

On a long-haul flight, paying a little more and traveling comfortably in a seat with more legroom or care service may be preferable.

Documents

Time is the most important thing when traveling. The earlier you book a flight, the cheaper it will be. By checking your documents early, you'll have more time to organize them. Make sure, for example, that your passport is valid. You will need more than six months left on your passport in many countries.

In addition, check if a visa is necessary even if you have been to your destination before since their immigration policy may have changed. In some countries, you can apply for a visa electronically, but in others, you must go to the consulate or embassy in person. The process can take weeks.

Before leaving your home, ensure you have the documentation in order.

Take a photo of the passport. Then save it to your phone and cloud using a password, so if you need it when you are away from home, you can find it easily.

The suitcase

Although it is basic advice, we tend to ignore it. Do not travel with excess baggage. Remember to pack only necessary items and forget about things you might not even use. Be sure to select clothing that can be combined. Choose footwear that is appropriate for the weather (and comfortable), and take accessories and technology items you won't find at the destination and might need. And if you're going overseas, don't forget your phone charger and adapter for that country.

Once you are sure about what you are taking with you, try to place everything in the suitcase in a way that takes up as little space as possible.

Bank and money

Although it may seem silly initially, the increase in identity theft is a serious threat, so it is worth telling your bank or credit card issuer that you will be traveling.

Additionally, it is always a good idea to notify your credit card company when traveling since some even offer free health coverage.

Finally, it's important to know the local currency and whether credit cards are accepted where you are traveling to.

Telephone strategy

Find out about your company's telephony conditions if you travel outside your country. To avoid unpleasant surprises when you receive your bill, check the roaming rates and follow the operator's instructions. Getting a local SIM card for your phone may be a good idea if your travel plans do not involve frequent travel. You can often purchase one online in advance. Using online messaging services like Zoom and whatsapp can be a great choice.

Health

Finding out in advance about the health system of the destination and where you can go is necessary. If you have health insurance, check what cover it includes abroad. Read the small print; you can get more than one shock. Health is expensive in many countries and poor in others. An insurance that covers all the guarantees and saves your trip can save your economy. If you live in Europe and will be traveling to another European country, apply for a free E111 form.

In terms of health, we need to consider our destination's policy. Find out in advance what vaccinations and health conditions are required for admission.

Finally, do not assume that abroad you will find common medicines with the same ease as here. They may be cheaper, infinitely more expensive, or they simply do not exist. Just in case, prepare your first aid kit.

Check the weather forecasts

This is not a minor matter, a few days before your trip, check the weather forecast. Plan ahead.

Free tours

Today, many tourist cities worldwide offer "free" tours you can find and book online. This type of tour is nice since the guides are usually locals who not only know the history and interesting facts about the place but also know where to eat and how to move around (and they share that information with the group). While they are not free, you just need to tip your guide at the end of the tour to rate his work.

What you need to know about social media

As long as we utilize them wisely, these digital channels will positively impact our lives. Therefore, to improve our relationship with Social Media, here are some tips to help us make the most of them and take advantage of all they offer.

Put down your phone

In the last few years, mobile phone usage has gone from 33% to 50.1%, i.e., half of the time spent online is through mobile devices. In this sense, the mobile is the main means of access to social networks. Be aware of how much time you spend on your phone. When you are old, one thing you'll never wish that you spent more time on your phone scrolling through social media!

Work on technological independence

Technological dependence is a real issue today. There are approximately 8.6 accounts on social networks per person around the world, and most are accessed through mobile devices.

Most people can't go more than an hour without looking at their phones, with 61% saying they check them first in the morning and the last thing at night.

The key to becoming more independent of technology is understanding what works best for you and your health and daily routine. There are endless options, like turning off your phone earlier to spend more time with friends or turning it on later to read something you enjoy while eating breakfast.

Limit the use of social networks.

Be aware of how much time you spend on social media. According to statistics, the average user of social networks spends two hours and twenty-four minutes per day on social networks. As an effective way to limit the amount of time the user spends on social networking sites, the time limit can be activated by social networks on the mobile device so that the user is more aware of how much time he wasted on his rambling before.

Follow quality accounts

You should ensure that your time on social media is spent on things that genuinely interest you, not on what is just noise. On social networks, become discerning with the accounts they follow. Remove accounts that make you feel sad or angry, or waste a lot of your time.

Identify the real stories

You should be aware that social media only displays a small part of a person and that reality is often much different. Many people believe that what is published on social media encompasses the entire life of influencers and brands. But, in reality, they show only a small portion of their daily lives. To avoid feeling frustrated when comparing their life with yours, you must be aware of this.

Use social media to get inspired and connect with others

Social networks allow you to discover new ideas, and ways of seeing and acting. These new social networks provide a source of inspiration for users by letting them imitate, add, and create content from original videos of their role models. Tik Tok videos, for example, receive an average of 17 billion views per month. This video social network has the highest social media engagement rate per post.

For brands, however, it is a new way to advertise their products and services more intimately than with a traditional ad. Pinterest has also become a great window for users who discover a large network of environments and trends they can duplicate in reality.

Engage friends and family via social media

With the advent of mobile phones, mobile networks have become the means of communication between friends and family. Mobile phones are used 70% by people to communicate with their closest friends and family through applications, social networks, or calls. Most mobile users only communicate via instant messaging applications or social networks. Social media platforms offer an immediacy that would otherwise be lacking.

Be empathic

With the pandemic, we have seen the need to support one another. It has demonstrated how vulnerable we are as a species, no matter our status, ethnicity, nationality, or sex.

We are all human, and we all have stories to tell. Understanding this is key to being responsible on social media. We can be proactive, assertive, and empathetic instead of joining the hate, ridicule, and criticism sweeping the world.

Conclusion

As children and teenagers, we were usually told where to go and what to do, by our parents, by our teachers in school and by adults. We didn't have a lot of choices. Instead there was a path we were expected to follow. Now as an adult, our lives are very different! And with the tips and strategies in this book you are now prepared to take on the world!

You've learned how to find a job, fix your car, live away from home and manage your money effectively. You understand how important it is to eat healthy, take care of your body, wear SPF and exercise.

You've discovered why it's good to make more money than you spend, make new friends to enrich your life, maybe even start your own business!

One of the most important lessons I learned in my life was to follow my gut and do more of what I love. If you are in a situation where your gut is saying something is off... listen to what your body is telling you. And that goes for a house share, a job or a night out in the city.

Figure out what you love. If you love art, don't give it up. Maybe you need an office job to pay the bills, but follow your dreams and keep painting on the weekends.

I truly hope that reading this book has greatly benefited you and helped you have great success and happiness in life as an adult. You can quickly implement the lessons you learned in your daily life and notice the positive effects.

Before you go, I have a small request to make. I would really appreciate it if you could review this book and share your lessons learned. Doing so will help me a lot in getting this book out to other young adults who can benefit from the tips and strategies I have shared.

We only get one chance to live our lives. Dream big and don't have any regrets.

You've got this!

Enjoy the next book in this series:

THE
COLLEGE LIFE
SURVIVAL
GUIDE
FOR GIRLS

Matilda Walsh

References

Hu, Y., Shmygelska, A., Tran, D., Eriksson, N., Tung, J. Y., & Hinds, D. A. (2016). GWAS of 89,283 individuals identifies genetic variants associated with self-reporting of being a morning person. *Nature communications, 7*(1), 1-9.

Made in the USA
Middletown, DE
21 December 2022

20060129R00116